WRITERS
NORTHWEST
HandBook

7th Edition

A Reference Guide for Northwest
Writers, Teachers, Publishers and Librarians

■

Publishers & Resources Directory

■

Essays, How-To Articles, Tips

D1739165

Media Weavers, *L.L.C.*

Copyright © 2003 Media Weavers, L.L.C.

Published by
Media Weavers, L.L.C.
P.O. Box 86190
Portland, OR 97286-0190

Designed by Donnelleigh S. Mounce, Graphic Design Studio, LLC

Printed in the United States of America

Media Weavers, L.L.C.
  Writers Northwest Handbook / edited by Media Weavers, L.L.C.
  ISBN 0-9647212-6-0
  1. Title   2. Reference   3. Writing   4. Northwest

Table of Contents

Introduction

We at Media Weavers are extremely pleased to present the Seventh Edition of the *Writers Northwest Handbook*. Its scope has been streamlined from earlier editions and we hope that the changes help you to be even more successful in pursuing your writing opportunities.

The purpose of the Handbook is two-fold. Its first section contains articles to inspire the writer and the second section provides pragmatic, support tools for achieving individual writing goals.

Part one contains representative categories of types of writing. Prominent authors share insights to guide you in your choice of writing style.

Whether you choose to write poetry, humor, science fiction, movie scripts, children's literature, mysteries or romances, these experts offer suggestions and inspiration to help you succeed.

Many of the authors featured in this section share with you the thrill of their first success, whether it was the publication of a first novel, screenplay or magazine article. We realize that the majority of the readers of this handbook are on the path to a first success and understand that achieving a first goal contains its own euphoria. Careers of the authors featured in the handbook have flourished from that time but always their first-time elation remains.

Part two gives you a wealth of options to help improve your writing, to effectively share your writing with others, and to market your writing. The database in this section provides the latest updates on book publishers, periodicals, newspapers, writers' organizations, contests, classes and conferences.

The *Writers Northwest Handbook* provides wise counsel. We wish you the best in using this remarkable tool.

Acknowledgements

Continuing the tradition, this handbook is dedicated to writers and the writing community. We thank the writers who contributed to this edition and are proud to share with you the best in Northwest writing along with helpful counsel and encouragement. Also we acknowledge the support of librarians, bookstore owners, literary agents, publishers, editors and advertisers — without whom, this book would not be possible.

Others have provided inspiration and support and we thank you:

Bob Howard who continuously provided expertise in almost everything – accounting, data base and research.

Editorial assistance: Sally Petersen

Design/Publication/Printing assistance: Donnelleigh S. Mounce, Diane Wagner

Advertisement assistance: Roberta Trahan

Media Weavers: the four people who make up the corporation that published this handbook — Publisher Marlene Howard, Poetry Editor Judith Massee, Book Editor Jennifer McCord and Editor at Large Joleen Colombo

The Spirit Within Good Books
Remarks: Oregon Book Awards
By John Daniel

I'd like to talk about this cultural thing — sometimes offensive, sometimes delighting, sometimes worthless, sometimes priceless — we call the book. As I was growing up in the 1950s, books were all around our house. Many kinds of books, from nice sets of Shakespeare and Francis Parkman, to early coffee-table books such as *The Family of Man*, to books on baseball and the "Freddy the Pig" stories my brother and I loved, to cheap paperback novels with lurid covers — lurid for the 1950s, anyway. It was commonplace to see my parents reading, my father in his maple rocker, my mother in the Morris chair or on the sofa. I grew up understanding that reading books, to me, was about more than reading. I liked to touch them, hold them, look at them arrayed on shelves.

> *Some people judge writing by how it sounds or looks. I judge it by how it smells.*

Once when I preferred to be alone I got rid of Bobby Bradley, my best friend, by feigning an avid interest in Macauley's *History of England*. The text did not engross me, but the book itself did. I liked the grainy paper, the feel of the rough fore-edges of the pages. I liked the hard gray covers, embossed with opulent lettering. I liked the substantial heft in my hands.

And I loved the smell, both musty and fresh, that filled my nose when I buried it in the book's open spine. How many of you like to sniff books? I know I'm not alone in this. A poet you may know of, a fellow named William Stafford, once claimed that he could find his way around the Lewis & Clark College library just by the smell of the books. "Books from Britain smell different from American books," he said. And he said, in his gently radical way, "Some people judge writing by how it sounds or looks. I judge it by how it smells. I want that total experience of language."

An earlier radical, Henry David Thoreau, wrote in his journal one day in 1850, "A truly good book is something as wildly natural and primitive, mysterious and marvelous, ambrosial and fertile, as a fungus or lichen." He was referring to the ideas and spirit of a good book, the wild, uncivilized thinking that delights us in *Lear* or the *Iliad*, but the sensory gusto of his small ode entitles us to suspect, at least, that Thoreau was a book-sniffer too.

A few have gone further than sniffing. At Stanford in the 1980s I made the casual acquaintance of Ian Watt, the great Conrad scholar, now dead. Ian Watt, in World War Two, was one of the British prisoners of war who built the bridge over the river Kwai. In the squalor and privation of the prison camp, he had managed to retain — appropriately — an edition of Dante's *Inferno*. Someone else had a store of moldy tobacco. No one had a pipe or paper. Which would it be, then — the solace of one of the great artistic achievements of the human imagination, or the comfort of an occasional smoke? Ian Watt memorized the *Inferno*, one page at a time, then tore the page from the book and ripped it into as many rolling papers as it would make. With his cohorts in slavery, he took the warmth of paper and ink into his lungs, and Dante Alighieri into his mind and heart.

A writer, I suspect, wants not just to write books. A writer wants to be a book.

"Book." The word itself has a heft and grain and smell in its own history. "Book" is directly related to "beech," as in beech tree, with an original sense of "beechwood sticks on which runes were carved." That early book must have been a handy thing. Besides self-edification, it could by used to bang robbers over the head, to lean on when tired, to start a fire when cold, even to sniff for its scent. Worthless, though, for pressing flowers, resting a coffee mug on, or riffling with the fingers just for the pleasure.

No one knows all that goes in to the making of an avid reader, but attraction to books as physical things surely plays some part. And no one knows all that goes in to the making of a writer, but — along with the mother complex, the poor social skills, the compulsive exhibitionism, the boundless ego and the perverse unwillingness to work a real job — along with those factors and more, a physical attraction to books must figure. A writer, I suspect, wants not just to write books. A writer wants to be a book.

In either case, if we're still to have readers and writers some decades from now, we had better hope that young people today are relishing the subtle scent of a warm computer and the aroma of pages freshly run off at Kinko's. The book and the process of publishing the book, after a long period of relative stasis, are undergoing an evolutionary spurt these days. Changes are happening, and happening fast.

There was a time when a book began life as a manuscript, and the edited manuscript was sent out for typesetting and printing. Now, a book may still exist early on as a manuscript, but it's probably encoded on a computer disk before it leaves the author's study. The book-to-be has become an electronic parcel which, after editing, can go right to the printer. But printing and paper are expensive. Holding printed books in warehouses and on bookstore shelves is expensive, due to various punitive, anti-entrepreneurial, un-American fees and taxes. Why not let the electronic parcel sit weightlessly, spacelessly and costlessly on the World Wide Web, and when someone wants to buy it, *then* print a copy.

This is called print-on-demand; it's happening now, and the product isn't bad. You get a book that looks much like a conventional trade paperback, the paper a little thinner, the cover art not as sharp. In two years, my editor tells me, you won't be able to tell a print-on-demand book from the real thing, and the two or three weeks it now takes to receive the book you order will telescope down to a few days, maybe even a few hours.

But what's the big deal? Right now you can walk into Broadway Books or Powell's or Looking Glass or Twenty-third Avenue or any other good store and walk out in minutes with the book you wanted, or walk out with that book and half a dozen you didn't know you wanted in a mere hour. Or, if you're handy with a mouse, you can click around cyberspace for a few minutes and receive your book from a dot.com in three or four days.

The benefit of print-on-demand (and as an unreconstructed neo-Luddite it pains me to acknowledge that there might be a benefit) may accrue indirectly to readers by accruing first to writers — writers such as many of us in this hall tonight and in this hall in other years, writers who do not enjoy a commercial success commensurate with their artistic achievement. (Or better, as I would tell a freshman English student who had written that sentence, good writers whose books don't sell.) By reversing the production model from print-then-distribute to distribute electronically then print on demand, the publisher relieves itself of the major up-front expense of printing and housing and shipping, and may therefore find it more plausible to keep midlist authors, and important but slow-selling back-list titles, in print. It is to be hoped.

But a more drastic development is occurring. The electronic parcel, capable critter that it is, can live without ink and paper entirely. It can be down loaded into a device about the size of a very old transistor radio or a large hardcover book, something with a name like *Sony Reader* or *RocketBook*, and on command will turn itself into print on a lighted screen. This is called, predictably, an e-book. Pretty snazzy. I wanted to smell one, but my local Radio Shack had none to show me. I am, however acquainted with computers.

There is a computer in my house and it has no discernable smell. I sit before it sometimes for long periods, coerced by editors, publishers and friends who have no tolerance for technological antiquity. I eye its screen dubiously the whole time I work. The best and highest use of an electronic screen, in my opinion, is for watching Barry Bonds or Edgar Martinez swing a baseball bat. *That* is why God gave us screens.

I don't want to read a book on a screen, even a screen I can lift about in my hands or prop on my chest in bed. Nor do I want to write a book on a screen. It's a pathetic bit of posturing, but when I write I want to make an impression on paper. Whether by pencil or pen or my archaic electric typewriter (which no one knows how to fix anymore when it breaks down.) I want to know that when I have written, say, the word "that," that I have accomplished at least that. It may vanish upon revision, it may turn out to have been a misbegotten or superfluous "that," but at the moment of conception there it is, branded on the page, and I am committed to it, and it, I believe, is committed to me.

I can't feel that way about "that," on a computer screen. I'm not even sure about the preposition — is it on the screen? *In* the screen? *Behind* the screen? Where and what exactly is that "that'? It is a tenuous thing, no more substantial than one of those quantum particles that physicists say are capable at any instant of dodging into or out of existence. It is a fundamentally equivocal "that." It burdens its author with the kind of

THE SPIRIT WITHIN GOOD BOOKS

discomforting question recently asked of a sitting American president. Do you have relations with that "that," or do you not?

I do not.

But forgive me, please, my rantish digression. For better or for worse, the e-book is at large among us, and according to my editor, it will find its appropriate uses. Here may be one. You're to travel to England, say, and you want to have with you two or three guidebooks, a history (maybe Macauley's) a book on Druids and stone circles, a field guide to British birds, works of Wordsworth and Hardy and others. Instead of schlepping all that book mass, you download the electronic essence of each into a portable *RocketBook* and summon each as you need it by tapping a few keys. Or maybe it will respond to your voice: "Come, Wordsworth, join me on my ramble!"

I have now a library of nearly nine hundred volumes, over seven hundred of which I wrote myself. . . .

I do have to acknowledge that the physicality I so love about books does make for a lot of weight, as all of us are reminded when we move and must pack all those books into all those boxes and — with luck — get someone younger to carry them. And a writer, of course, in addition to the poundage of the books he reads, must at times bear the burden of books he has written.

To turn this talk toward its perhaps overdue close, I give you, in his words, the afternoon of October 28, 1853, in the life of Henry David Thoreau: "For a year or two past, my publisher, falsely so called, has been writing from time to time to ask what disposition should be made of the copies of *A Week on the Concord and Merrimack Rivers* still on hand, and at last suggesting that he had use for the room they occupied in his cellar. So I had them all sent to me here, and they have arrived today by express, filling the man's wagon — 706 copies out of an edition of 1,000 which I bought of Munroe four years ago and have been ever since paying for, and have not quite paid for yet. . . . They are something more substantial than fame, as my back knows, which has borne them up two flights of stairs to a place similar to that to which they trace their origin. I have now a library of nearly nine hundred volumes, over seven hundred of which I wrote myself . . . I can see now what I write for, the result of my labors."

Surely not one of the best days of Henry's life, but he takes it with grace. And then, at the end of the same journal entry, he writes a sentence I find very moving: "Nevertheless, in spite of this result, sitting beside the inert mass of my works, I take up my pen tonight to record what thought or experience I may have had, with as much satisfaction as ever."

All of the people we honor tonight know exquisitely well that sitting down in solitude to the work at hand, whatever the fortunes of their careers in the world. The book can be found in paper and ink between covers, but it does not live there, and neither does it live in backlit type on a screen. Its native habitat is that wild solitude in which the writer turns and turns again to the enticing, vexing, elusive and necessary work. So long as writers keep doing that, and so long as others seek to enter that solitude through the mystery we call reading, the book, whatever its physical form, will survive and thrive. We of what Wallace Stegner called "the great community of recorded human experience" will continue this remarkable conversation we are having, across vast lengths of time and distance, about who we are, about where we are, about what we have known, and feared, and loved, and hoped for, about how our lives have mattered.

John Daniel is the author of Oregon Book Award winners Looking After *and* The Trail Home, *and most recently,* Winter Creek: One Writer's Natural History. *He presented these ideas in a speech to writers at the 2000 Oregon Book Awards ceremonies in Portland, Ore.*

Funny You Should Write That!

By Gordon Kirkland

It's often been said that humor is one of the most difficult genres to tackle. Put simply, writing humor is only a two-step process — think of something funny, and write it down. Most people find that the write-it-down step is much easier than the think-of-something-funny, but until they've mastered the first step, knowing how to write doesn't come in all that handy.

Identifying what constitutes humor is nearly impossible. Aristotle tried to define humor. Sigmund Freud tried to identify the purpose of humor. Even Darwin got into the act. None of them could come up with a clear definition of what is, and what is not, funny. Something that might make a Howard Stern fan laugh might not be considered very funny at all by one of Billy Graham's followers. Therefore, the humorist's first commandment is 'Know thy audience.'

Humor is both a genre in its own right, and an important ingredient in many other genres. William Shakespeare wrote comedies, tragedies and romances. Even in the most tragic of tales, he knew the importance of inserting a humorous scene every so often to bring the audience some comic relief, from all the death, deceit and unrequited love in the rest of the play.

To many people humor is synonymous with jokes. While joke writing is a subsection of the genre, and a potentially lucrative one, it would be a mistake to confuse the ability to tell a joke with the ability to write humor. We've all met people who are "quick with a joke." More often than not they are simply repeating, perhaps embellishing, a joke that someone else told them. You don't need a sense of humor to tell a joke. You just need to be good at memorizing short passages.

There are three important elements to humor writing. They can be used together or on their own with equal success. These are:

- The Unexpected or Surprise Twist;
- Creating a Sense of Superiority; and,
- Playing on Incongruities.

The Unexpected or Surprise Twist

Humor is often built on surprise. Creating an image in the readers' mind, and then completely destroying it with a sudden change in direction is an excellent way to evoke laughter. For example, the following passage is from a piece I wrote about something I had to give up after breaking my spine:

> "I miss the feel of hot, sweaty flesh, pounding rhythmically beneath me, and the sounds of heavy breathing and snorting as I go up and down — at times barely able to avoid falling off. I miss the rush it gave me as it forces adrenaline through my system. It wasn't that I experienced it all that often, and frankly, I wasn't very good at it, but every time I did it I had a really good time. Had I known that I'd have to stop doing it, I would have done it a lot more when I could. That's why I find it hard to believe that there are people out there who have no desire to even try it. I'm sure some of you just take doing it for granted. I did, and of course now I wish I hadn't.
>
> "Yes, I sure do miss the joys of riding a horse."

The first paragraph is ambiguous enough to create the impression that I am talking about another, enjoyable activity. By going into a lot of detail, I strung the reader along, even further down the wrong path. The short, kicker paragraph provides the surprise by quickly letting them know that what they are thinking is way off base. Had I introduced the idea of horseback riding in the opening, the reader would have created an entirely different image in their minds about the 'hot sweaty flesh pounding rhythmically beneath me," and the surprise would have been eliminated.

Creating a Sense of Superiority

Much so called humor writing is based on creating a sense of superiority, in the reader, the author, or both. Ethnic, racial and sexist jokes play on creating a sense of superiority. While political correctness might keep us away from writing that sort of material, it is still possible to use a sense of superiority without offending people. Slapstick comedy, practical jokes and embarrassing the key subject all rely on using the reader or viewer's sense of superiority over the person at the butt of the joke.

When I speak to writers' groups about writing humor, I start them off by asking them to think of their most embarrassing moment. Odds are at the time, they might have said, "Someday I might laugh at this situation." Sharing those stories entertain the reader, partially by giving them permission to feel a little bit superior to you, the writer. For example:

"I opened the refrigerator, and what to my wondering eyes should appear, but a snack item that my sons had obviously overlooked. There, on a side plate, wrapped with cellophane, was some leftover meat paté. I spread a generous helping on a cracker, and quickly discovered why no one had eaten the rest of this culinary delight. It tasted terrible. I re-wrapped it, and returned it to the refrigerator, because I know that there is one person in this household who can eat disgusting things like broccoli without gagging, so I assumed the paté belonged to her.

"When I mentioned my unappetizing experience to my dear, kind, loving wife, she gave me one of those deer-in-the-headlights looks and said, 'You didn't…'

"She tried to tell me I had eaten cat food, but I pointed out that the cat food was clearly visible on another shelf.

"'Dear, she said, already starting to laugh, 'I put cat food on that plate, and mixed in the anti-flea medicine to make it easier to give it to her.'"

In this case, the reader's sense of superiority is played in two ways. First they can laugh, at the thought of someone eating cat food, and secondly by enjoying the other person's misfortune. (In case you're wondering, I had no trouble with fleas that whole season.)

Playing on Incongruities

Humor is often developed by joining two or more subjects that don't seem to belong together. This might be achieved by creating a seemingly improbable action such as childlike behavior in an adult. It can also be developed by having the subject display an emotion that is the opposite to what might be expected in the location or setting. Incongruity is a device that opens the door for another comic device — exaggeration.

"After our second child was born, my wife and I discussed the two options of permanent birth control. . . . I lost. (Although I still say my wife cheated on the tie breaking arm wrestle.) In a visit to my doctor, who, until that moment, I had considered a friend, we were shown pictures of what the procedure involved. My wife seemed to enjoy them. I, on the other hand, sat in the fetal position, in a corner, with my hands over my ears, singing, 'La! La! La! I can't hear you. . . .'"

Some readers, mostly those who haven't seen the pictures described in the above passage, might find it incongruous, that a fully grown adult would behave the way I did. Obviously, the images invoked fear, even though I was in the relative safety of a doctor's office, especially when you consider that I thought he was my friend. I also have to admit that I exaggerated a little when I wrote that passage. My wife actually won the tie breaking arm wrestle fair and square.

Finding A Topic

The world really is a pretty funny place. Often, when we get caught up in the events of our daily lives, we miss a lot of the humor that surrounds us. Taking a step back and allowing yourself to be a bit more observant, will open your eyes to a lot of funny topics. Be careful. You might become tempted to write about anything and everything that strikes you as funny. Focusing on a selected topic or small group of topics will make it much easier to develop your comedic voice, a specific audience and a sense of security in your ability to consistently make your readers laugh. Two common topics are politics and family life.

Politics

Obviously, the political arena is filled with opportunities for humorists. Comedians rely heavily on political humor, as do satirists, and commentators. It's topical, anyone who reads a newspaper or watches television will have some knowledge of the subject, and it's filled with incongruities. Politicians seem to have a knack for getting themselves into situations that provide a plethora of material for the humorists who focus on this subject area.

"The Houston Chronicle described Canadian Prime Minister Jean Chretien as 'an irreverent and irascible man who once punched a heckler.' As a Canadian I was deeply offended by that description. Our leader is an irreverent and irascible man who once put a heckler in a choke hold, but he didn't punch the man."

This statement uses both surprise and incongruity. The reader expects that I will complain about the entire description of the Canadian leader, not just the fact that the newspaper got the assault facts wrong. The incongruity is obvious, who would ever guess that the leader of a country would put a heckler in a choke hold?

Family Life

> . . .I often refer to my sons as my "grocery-sucking appetites on legs."

Humorists who focus on family life tend to look closely at the little situations that occur in everyone's life, but that often go unnoticed. Situations that you might find frustrating in your own life might seem quite humorous when someone else writes about facing the same frustration. Parents of teenagers are often exasperated by the quantity of food their offspring can consume, who only to return to the kitchen a half an hour later, claiming to be starving. In my weekly column, I often refer to my sons as my "grocery-sucking appetites on legs."

"You know you're in trouble when you run out of food before you've finished unloading the groceries from the car."

The above statement uses a bit (in my family's case a very little bit) of exaggeration and incongruity. It also draws a bit on a surprise kicker — an unusually fast consumption of groceries — and it lets the reader feel a bit superior because they've never had it quite that bad.

The Marketplace for Humor

Early in my career I was told by a literary agent that I must be some kind of idiot to think that there is any market for humor. I could either take this person's word for it, or assume that Erma Bombeck, Dave Barry, Lewis Grizzard and Garrison Keillor weren't really all idiots. Thankfully, I chose to believe in my fellow writers. Yes Virginia, there is a market for humor.

Community Newspapers

Small community newspapers have launched more than a few humor writers' careers. The more relaxed style of a community newspaper makes it a good proving ground for the emerging writer. While the pay might not be the greatest, they do provide writers with two of the most necessary tools for marketing — publication credits, and sample clippings.

Daily Newspapers

Selling to a daily newspaper is a bit more difficult, and the pay isn't necessarily that much better. Currently I receive between $20.00 and $150.00 per column from the dailies that carry my work. The range is based on a number of factors including circulation, and the economic situation of the newspaper's market region. As you can see, feeding a couple of grocery-sucking appetites on legs necessitates getting published in several newspapers each week.

Consumer Magazines

Writing humor for the magazine market is more lucrative than for newspapers, but it takes a lot more work to make the sale. Still, many of the *Writers Digest* Top 100 magazine markets for new writers list humor as one of their genres. Probably the best known of these markets is *Reader's Digest*. It purchases hundreds of short (200 words or less) humorous pieces every year.

Trade Publications

Trade publications are often good markets for short humor pieces relating to the specific industry or profession. There are even trade magazines which are completely dedicated to humor. One of these, a Canadian magazine for doctors called *Stitches*, has been a frequent market for my articles.

In addition to columns and feature articles, all four of the above publication types are excellent markets for fillers. A filler is a very short item that the editor can use to fill up a small space left blank at the end of a longer article. Newspapers tend to look for more current or topical fillers, while magazines are more open to material that isn't as time sensitive.

Greeting Cards

If you have a knack for really short pieces that pack a punch, the greeting card market might be right for you. This industry has an almost insatiable demand for new and funny ways of looking at familiar topics like birthdays, anniversaries, or quadruple bypass surgery.

Other

Other markets for humor include radio and TV shows, stand-up comedians and even corporations seeking to inject a sense of humor into an otherwise dull and boring speech by the CEO.

Getting There Is Half The Fun

The learning process involved in writing humor is an enjoyable one. I recommend that would-be humorists spend a lot of time reading what has already been written, listening carefully to comedians' routines and observing the passages of time for those unique moments that draw a humorous response.

There are a number of excellent writers who have made humor their primary genre. Obviously, I am a big fan of the late Lewis Grizzard. Of course Erma Bombeck was another great inspiration when I was getting started. In addition, I recommend going back and reading everything from Shakespeare's comedies like "Twelfth Night," to the writings of people like James Thurber and Stephen Leacock. Each of these writers has taught me something about the use of words, timing, and the subtleties of making people laugh with me, at me and hopefully at themselves.

It is also critical that you keep up to date with current events. I read at least two newspapers each day. Writer's block hits humorists too. Small, insignificant items in a newspaper have often triggered the idea for my weekly column.

Listening to comedians is another important tool for the humor writer. I've picked up a lot of ideas about timing and how to draw the reader into the story from people like Jay Leno, Jeff Foxworthy and Tim Allen.

Humor writing contains many of the same elements that are the basis of all good writing. Most colleges and universities offer extension courses in creative writing. I strongly recommend taking as many of them as you can. I'd also recommend attending writers' conferences and critique groups to further hone your style. Through them I have learned a great deal that has helped me develop as a writer, and I have also learned valuable lessons about dealing with the publishing industry.

Finally, I want to point out that life as a humor writer is marvelous therapy. It is really difficult to become depressed when you are focusing your energies on making yourself and others laugh.

Gordon Kirkland writes the syndicated humor column, Gordon Kirkland At Large, *which is a regular feature in many newspapers in Canada and the United States. He is also the author of* Justice Is Blind – and Her Dog Just Peed In My Cornflakes *(Harbour Publishing). It was awarded the prestigious 2000 Stephen Leacock Award of Merit. Kirkland is now working on two new books. He lives near Vancouver, British Columbia, with his wife, two sons and the dumbest dog to ever get lost on a single flight of stairs.*

Literary Magazines:
The Writer's Friend
By Dennis Held

They are the unvarnished murmurings of the human heart: the poetry and prose submissions of the hopeful writer-to-be, sent off to a distant big-city literary magazine, the manuscripts forced to languish for months unread in a cardboard box until glanced at by some cynical uncaring editor, deemed unworthy and returned unceremoniously with a form rejection letter, without so much as a howdy-do. It's the heartless, unrewarding world of the literary magazine. If you want to play, you better toughen up, cowboy — there's a world of hurt out there, with your name on it.

OR . . . You do a little research, you find a few magazines in your region that publish the kind of writing you like to read, you send off your first fragile efforts, they come back with a nice note, telling which of your poems came closest for that particular editor, who encourages you to submit again, and you do, and one day your mailbox brings you an acceptance letter, that small sparkle of goodwill that helps you keep going to the next level in that long journey you're on to becoming a writer. And years later, after you've sold your first novel, or won a prize for your second book of poems, you'll look back at that first publication in a small but attractive journal as the carrot that kept you moving forward just when your spirit was flagging and you were thinking about chucking the whole writing thing once and for all.

Literary magazines provide all sorts of services to writers — and to readers. They often provide the first exposure for the writers who will someday be household names. They also provide an important part of the web of community that holds writers together, linking readers and writers and providing a note of affirmation in a culture that would too-often like to ignore its artist, especially those who challenge convention.

Definition

This definition could get tricky, but in general, a literary magazine, or journal, is a publication that comes out regularly, and contains literary writing: usually, a combination of poetry, fiction and nonfiction.

Some journals include book reviews, scholarly writing, visual art, you name it, but the focus is most often on contemporary, shorter works — poems, stories, novel excerpts and first-person creative nonfiction.

By "literary writing," I mean work that exhibits a freshness and originality in all its elements — word choice, structure, syntax and the like — without sounding strained or self-conscious. It pays attention to sound, to rhythm, to vowel-consonant interaction. It uses the specific to illustrate the general, thereby connecting in a deep and meaningful way with the emotional world of a wide range of readers.

There — that's all you need to do, and your work will start appearing in better magazines near you.

Writing Opportunities

I believe in taking a litero-regional approach to magazines: find out which ones in your area are doing good work, and submit to them. And by all means, subscribe to them. (I don't just say this because I have been the faculty advisor to the *Talking River Review*, 500 8th Ave., Lewiston, ID 83501, subscriptions $12 annually, either!)

You should check these magazines out, face to face, at a library if possible, or drop them a note and a few sheckles and ask for a recent back issue. ($5 usually does the trick . . .) If you find yourself nodding your head and smiling pleasantly while reading, send your work to that journal.

How to Send

Include a brief — very brief, a few sentences — cover letter. Here's what I usually say: Dear Blank, (get the name of the appropriate editor if possible, or just say dear poetry editor), I have enclosed the following poems: "Title," "Title" and "Title." A LINE OF BIO HERE — I have recently published work in *Dogbreath Magazine*, and have work forthcoming from *Slugpouch Monthly*. Thanks for your consideration.

Best regards, YOUR NAME.

That's it. Note the italics, and note that periods and commas always go inside of quotation marks — don't let your first impression with an editor be a typo.

Include a self-addressed stamped envelope, and in your cover letter you might indicate if you want the work returned. The usual manuscript rules apply: double-space prose, one-inch margins, print on one side only, and your name should appear somewhere on each page — lower right is good, so it doesn't interfere with the reading of the work.

There's a lot of talk about simultaneous submissions. If you're sending out prose, you might want to send one story to a couple of magazines, maybe three, but I wouldn't do any more than that. Keep meticulous records, and if your work is accepted somewhere, immediately drop a note to the other magazines, withdrawing it from consideration. Be aware that some magazines will not consider simultaneous submissions, so you might want to write ahead for guidelines before submitting.

Poetry? I don't know — I usually send out batches of three to five poems, and it gets hard to keep track of everything if you're sending out multiple submissions. On the other hand, if it takes a magazine four months to send you a form rejection letter, you might want to keep a batch out at a couple of places simultaneously. Be aware that you risk an editor's wrath — and it is righteous wrath — if you withdraw a piece that was under consideration, had been past a few readers, had involved the editor in some time-consuming discussions . . . you get the drift.

Where to Go

Start by identifying some good publications in your region — say a four- or five-state area — and sending them your best work. And sure, go ahead, send your best work to the top-flight New York fancy-pants magazines, too. Who knows — you might get lucky and catch somebody's eye. A longish story in *The New Yorker* magazine could provide a $10,000 payday. But don't give up your day job, just yet. . . .

Best Bets

Look for magazines that have some stability — I've had work accepted by places that put out an issue or two, then folded their tents in the night, and disappeared. (That's the fate of most literary magazines, by the by. I was talking with a writer friend the other day who had come across a list of his first publications. He read off the names of about twenty of the magazines, and there were only two that I recognized — and they were both defunct.)

Your best bet for getting published, of course, is to continue to improve your writing. I once asked William Kittredge how I could get more of my work landed in magazines. He smiled a bit cruelly. "Write better," he said. (He'd seen some of *early* efforts, of course . . .) "Seriously though," he said, "what you have to do is increase the reader's emotional response to your work. And you do that by writing good, clear, solid sentences, and writing about something you give a shit about." So there you have it — the wisdom of one of the best in the business, and I ain't talking about me.

> *Your best bet for getting published, of course, is to continue to improve your writing.*

Take classes, go to conferences, go to workshops, write more letters, read more widely, get into a writing group with disciplined writers and push each other: there are a lot of ways to improve your writing. But finally, those who write well seem to write a lot. They make time for their writing, and for their reading, and they read good writers. You must learn to read like a writer before you can learn to write like a reader.

Literary magazines can help provide a vital link in your chain of becoming, and being, a writer. Support the journals in your area that support other writers, and everybody wins.

Dennis Held is a writer who teaches a Lewis-Clark State College in Lewiston Idaho.

Writing Literary Nonfiction
Or Stalking the Style With a Dozen Names
By Lisa Dale Norton

Everyone's trying it and everyone's bashing it. It clogs bestseller lists whiled it takes a thrashing on editorial pages. It's loved by readers, hated by reviewers and reviled by novelists. It's literary nonfiction.

Or creative nonfiction. Or how about memoir? The essay, perhaps? Or the literary essay? The personal essay? Travel writing? Could we say it was literary journalism? Whatever you call this form two things are true: it is popular and it confuses people. Witness this scene I experienced at a recent writing conference. A young woman posed a question to the room. "What is creative nonfiction?" her thin voice rose above the noise. Voices quieted, heads turned, shoulders shrugged.

"Why it's just an excuse to write fiction and call it true," one burly man wearing Reebok sandals and shorts called out.

"No, it's the essay," said another. "There are only three forms: fiction, poetry and the essay." This fellow punctuated the air with fingers like a conductor signaling an orchestra.

"I think it's a place where a person can do a lot of things," ventured a dark-haired woman. She had sad brown eyes above a saffron scarf. "But mostly it's about voice."

"So do I have to get my quotes absolutely right?" the young writer queried the Saffron woman.

"It's not journalism," she replied.

"But it's supposed to be true," the Reebok man responded . . . .

Here is the eternal dialogue concerning literary nonfiction. How shall we define this form? What qualities give literary nonfiction its familiar feel? Let me venture a definition.

Literary nonfiction borrows from many forms. It is an amalgam of techniques: reportage is borrowed from journalism, scene construction and character development is adopted from the novel, first-person narration is taken from the personal essay, and all are rolled into a compelling story complete with dramatic movement toward the recognition of some universal truth. That's a complicated way of saying: it's a story that keeps me turning pages late at night because I love the characters and the narrator, because I have to find out what's going to happen, and because I know the story is true. "Literary" implies something more, thought. It implies that the language is beautiful, that there is music to the words, like poetry, that the writing has rhythm, a depth greater than content alone. I come to literary nonfiction seeking a true story, an honest voice that compels me, teaches me, and language like some luscious fruit.

How did I get involved in literary nonfiction? I'd always had a knack for expressing myself on the page, ever since I was a kid writing letters to distant pen pals and bosom friends, and somehow by a dozen twists of fate, I found myself writing about the arts, after years of music study. I worked as an arts critic, after I earned my undergraduate degree, writing reviews of musical performances and theatrical shows. In graduate school I studied journalism and made my way to the writing of feature stories and news articles, but I soon found the shape of journalism restrictive, took to writing more expansive stories, could not keep myself from incorporating techniques my editor did not find appropriate for news.

I was on the trail of a

way of writing. . . .

Thank heavens I found literary journalism. The doors were thrown wide as I read Tracy Kidder, Joan Didion, John McPhee, Tom Wolfe, Bill Barich, Calvin Trillin, Richard Rhodes, Michael Herr, Jane Kramer, Hunter Thompson. I combined my interest in their work with a love of nature writing — the work of Annie Dillard, Bill Kittredge, Ann Zwinger, Bob Finch, Barry Lopez — and the growing body of women's stories I began to read, Books by: Patricia Hampl, Sue Hubbell, Terry Tempest Williams, Gretel Ehrlich, Teresa Jordan.

What began to rise inside me was a desire to tell stories about my life and the places I loved complete with character and scenes, travel adventures, reported facts, all in my voice. Call it what you like — I didn't care what it was called. I was on the trail of a way of writing and I moved in a direction, teaching myself how to do it, and never giving up.

Fifteen years later, in 1995 Picador USA purchased hardcover and trade paperback rights for my book *Hawk Flies Above: Journey to the Heart of the Sandhills.* In the fall of 1996 when the hardcover came out and the publisher printed the words "a memoir" on the front of the book, I knew it was a marketing decision. I knew the story was so much more. It was nature writing, environmental tract, personal essay, travel story and literary journalism. It was what many call creative non-fiction, what I call literary nonfiction — an amalgam of writerly techniques rolled into a story with dramatic action that the author narrates.

Unlike the young woman at the conference who sought a definition for creative nonfiction, though, I did not worry about what I was writing while I worked on my book. And that, *Dear Reader,* is exactly what I encourage you to do. Do not worry about what it is you are writing. Simply write. Pages upon pages. Write around and through, over and into the words and feelings and ideas you have, and somewhere in that soup of stuff will be your story. You are not going to find it, though, until you let yourself unfold a whole lot of schlock. And it will be hard to do even that if you are forever worrying about what form you are writing or debating with the all-too-ready crowd of critics who believe you are sullying literature's trinity: fiction, poetry or the essay.

So, how do you get started? Here are four steps for finding and writing your stories and joining the ranks of those of us who live and breathe literary nonfiction:

1) Pay attention to your life: what ideas, concepts, events, memories, places are you drawn to, passionate about?

2) Write about any ideas or images that present themselves as important. Is it your Aunt Catherine? Or the suburbs that encroach on your rural lifestyle? Your high school sweetheart you just can't get out of your heart and mind? Maybe you know exactly what it is you want to write about: that road trip you took in Africa 10 years ago, the Superfund site in your community, the barter currency your town is developing. Whatever it may be, write down the thoughts that come to you. Use short freewrites of 10 minutes if you feel resistance to this step. Everyone has 10 minutes — lingering over a cup of coffee, riding to work on the train in the morning, sitting with a loved one who is resting. Take 10 minutes and write down what's on your mind. And then do it again and again, until you believe you've written out all the thoughts and memories you have. Twenty to 25 of these short 10-minute pieces would be a good place to start. This gives you material to work with. I tell my students, "You wouldn't start to build a house without materials, would you?" So it is with the building of a piece of literary nonfiction. You need raw materials, and those are your initial stories — what you know, remember and wonder. Write it all down.

3) Then start to play with these short pieces. Read them over. See if you can find any reoccurring ideas? Don't get neurotic about the writing and start editing. Just go for the big picture, the overview. Ask yourself, does each short vignette explore the same place, or person? Perhaps they all seem to be circling around the joy you felt when you landed your first job, or the loss you felt when your grandmother died. Do certain stories seem to belong in a group together? Do they seem to be about the same topic? What is that topic? Keep pushing at the material in this way, asking yourself what it is you feel you are exploring — what topic or concept — until you can get it down to a word or short phrase. In my classes students have come up with words like: betrayal, loss of home, corporate greed, degradation of the environment, family, community.

Only through this kind of back and forth between a) writing out our images and thoughts; and b) grappling with the larger issues pulsing under those images and thoughts will you begin to find your way into the structure of the story. And structure is the heart of it all. In the end, you have to find a framework to hold the ideas and stories, a way of weaving together the scenes and narration and reportage. Structure, the architecture of a piece of literary nonfiction, rises organically out of what you are trying to say, and so only when you know what you are trying to say will you know where to start the story, where to go in the narrative, what to leave in, what to take out, and where to end the story. Structure and the central concept you are exploring go hand in hand in a piece of literary nonfiction.

4) To get at a structure keep writing down any new thoughts and experiences that pertain to your topic. Keep exploring the larger issue under your story through free writing, until finally a structure begins to present itself. I know this sounds lame, but it's the only true way you can let the story happen. As artists we're responsible for making ourselves available for the gift. So it is with structure and a piece of writing: you simply have to be there, make yourself available to the possibilities, and that happens when you mess around with your ideas and experiences in writing on the page. If you stick with it — writing, thinking, asking questions, gathering new information and writing about that — if you immerse yourself in the subject, the shape of the story will come.

It helps to read other writers, of course. But pay attention while you're reading. I'm always analyzing writing. Even if I read a whole book quickly, just for the story, if I love it and want to learn from it, I go back and read it a second time for craft. The margins of my books are riddled with notes to myself about what it is the writer is doing at each turn of the text. By this careful analysis I have learned a great deal about structure, I have learned how other authors put together literary nonfiction, whether it be a short magazine essay, like those that appear in the "Thoughts of Home" column in House Beautiful; a rambling personal piece in a literary journal like Creative Nonfiction; or a complete book on topics as diverse as cancer, horse racing, coming of age, killing and religious communities. Each has shown me the importance of building a one-of-a-kind structure to house the tale.

Structure and the central concept you are exploring go hand in hand. . . .

Certainly reading is an excellent way to learn about writing literary nonfiction, but there are plenty of good classes, too. In 1994 I founded Neahkahnie Institute in Manzanita on the coast of Oregon. We sponsor a year-long calendar of writing workshops exploring landscape and creativity, and each year I teach at least one class in literary nonfiction. My annual Writing Workshop for Women entitled "Writing Memoir," which falls within the larger category of literary nonfiction, is always a popular and lively weekend retreat. I also teach a small group manuscript workshop in literary nonfiction.

And all over the country more and more classes in nonfiction writing are springing up in academic communities. Journalism has always been a good grounding in the basics, but now you can find creative nonfiction classes in the English department, and offerings in community education programs are growing too. These latter classes usually have no prerequisites.

If college life doesn't fit your schedules, call a local writing organization or writing center — Richard Hugo House in Seattle, Mountain Writers Center in Portland, Log Cabin in Boise, to name a few — for a schedule of classes. These are usually taught by local luminaries, or itinerant authors on the road to promote a book. In addition, there are writing conferences all over the country during the summer where well-known writers and rising stars share their take on literary nonfiction. Two big conferences in the Northwest are the Willamette Writers Conference in Portland and the Pacific Northwest Writers Association Conference in Seattle, but there are many others, some quite intimate where you get personal attention, like Neahkahnie Institute or the Oregon Writers Colony. Read Poets & Writers magazine to get a feel for your options. But do your research to be sure you get the kind of learning experience that's right for you. Each conference has its own ambiance and style. Some can be quite competitive and beginning writers can get buried.

As far as marketing is concerned, literary nonfiction is hot. If you have a personal experience to share and you can find a compelling way to package the story, you'll no doubt find a market for your work — be it a magazine or publishing house. That is, if you never give up. Some things take time, and patience is not a virtue our culture teaches.

I have a scrap of newsprint taped to the top edge of my computer monitor. It is yellowed with age. It has lived on two different computers over my years as a writer, transferred gingerly from one to the other. I clipped the words from some article long forgotten. It is from the heart of a longer paragraph, and its goes like this: "...And I recalled the advice of Winston Churchill, who said the secret of success is never give up, never give up, never give up."

Lisa Dale Norton is the author of Hawk Flies Above: Journey to the Heart of the Sandhills. *For the past nine years Norton has lived in Manzanita on the coast of Oregon where she has served as Director of Neahkahnie Institute, which she founded in 1994. The Institute sponsors creative writing workshops and The Onion Peak Reading Series. Norton teaches writing at colleges and conferences nationwide. A graduate of Reed College and the University of Iowa, her latest book of narrative nonfiction,* Anatome of a Romance, *is forthcoming.*

Find a Real Job

By Marjorie Reynolds

I started writing again because I lost my job. I say *again*, because I had once worked as a newspaper reporter. As one accustomed to seeing my name on a page, I assumed the conversion to fiction would be easy — a lot easier than searching for a real job. With that combination of arrogance and naiveté, I was lucky to have sold a book at all. My advice to you is, "Go for the real job first." If that doesn't pan out and you can't resist the lure of creating a world you can manipulate and lose yourself in, resign yourself to writing fiction.

. . . with good intentions and sheer stubbornness you turn out a halfway decent result. . . .

It didn't take long for me to discover that novel writing is harder, more draining, more competitive, more discouraging, more unpredictable than anything else I've ever done — with the exception of raising children. At the same time, it has given me the biggest thrill I've ever known. When all goes well, I feel as if I've made the perfect three-point basketball shot, vaulted my way to an Olympic gold medal or won an eighty-mile marathon.

Authors often compare the process to childbirth, from conception to delivery, but I think it bears a stronger resemblance to raising kids. You make lots of mistakes along the way, but miraculously, with good intentions and sheer stubbornness you turn out a halfway decent result. You get what you put into it. Of course, you may have to abandon the hope of a Pulitzer or the National Book Award, just as most of us give up on a National Merit Scholarship and Harvard for our children, but that doesn't lessen the pleasure of the process.

In a dim room, facing a wall, I wrote my first novel, a loosely structured tome with very little action but plenty of angst and penetrating introspection. It didn't occur to me to try something shorter or less challenging. I hadn't penned a short story since college. I'd never written a poem, and my only experience with a journal dated back to junior high school. Although my genre of choice was mysteries when it came to reading, I decided to write a mainstream novel, one that might appeal to a cross-section of readers. To tell the truth, I wasn't sure I was clever enough to plot the twists and turns of a mystery, and I'd read very little of other genres, such as romance, science fiction, fantasy or horror.

I finished *Small Compensations* in about six months. Never mind that it was nothing more than a first draft. I honestly thought I'd written the great American novel. I was certain that if I sent the first two chapters to a dozen New York publishing houses, editors would hurry to phone me, asking me to FedEx the remaining chapters. I was euphoric with anticipation.

> *I took to my*
>
> *bed again.*

Not only did I not receive any calls, but 10 of the dozen publishers returned my packages unopened, accompanied by notes informing me they didn't read "unagented" fiction. The other publishers directly rejected the chapters with form letters.

In disappointment, I took to my bed for two days.

Finally, I pulled myself to my feet and began my search for a literary agent. For the uninitiated, a literary agent is a business person who has extensive contacts with editors and publishing houses, usually in New York City. She (or he) would read my novel, pass judgment on it and, if I were lucky, choose to take me on as a client and sell the book on my behalf.

I found a woman agent in Seattle who agreed to read my entire manuscript, while I eagerly awaited her verdict. She called to tell me it was "the bleakest, most disturbing, most unrelentingly depressing manuscript" she'd come across in years. She read it one night before she went to bed and found it so upsetting she couldn't fall asleep.

"You don't think it's a love story?" I asked in disbelief.

She didn't.

Not only did she not have one positive word to say about it, she made a point of noting she'd encountered far better writers. I took to my bed again.

Luckily, I met a creative writing professor at the University of Washington a few weeks later. He'd had twelve novels published, but he'd written twenty-four. I felt slightly better. I poured out the literary agent's discouraging litany and asked him what he thought I should do.

He regarded me with surprise. "Those sound like flattering words to me. She didn't say your novel was the blandest one she'd ever read. You upset her. You kept her awake at night. If I were you, I'd keep on writing."

It had never occurred to me to consider her remarks that way. I made some changes in the manuscript and sent it to several other agents. They too rejected it, but I saw a consensus in their replies. They liked my style of writing but not the story. I could change the story, I realized, much easier than I could change my style.

I set out to write another novel based on two things I knew well: a drive-in theater and a small Indiana town. But, this time, I treated the process as a learning experience. I took some classes and workshops, read books on the craft, joined a critique group and attended the Pacific Northwest Writers Conference. By that time, I knew the chances of getting my new novel in print would be slim. Only two percent of manuscripts submitted to agents and editors are ever published — a grim statistic designed to demoralize even the most tenacious.

Let me stop right here, and go off on an important tangent. I wanted to quit writing at this point. I realized I could spend the next 10 years spitting out words and produce nothing more than enough scrap paper to start a decent bonfire. I told myself I was foolish to spend my time pounding a computer keyboard in a dark room. This business was too hard, the competition too stiff, the rewards too meager (I'd read some other statistic about only a few hundred novelists in America making enough to live on). I was a sensitive person; I hated rejection. For God's sake, I didn't even like to write. That's why I had quit newspaper work.

"I spent six months writing this manuscript and look what I have to show for it," I wailed to a friend.

She shrugged. "I spent the same six months you did, and I've got nothing. So, you're ahead of me."

Like the professor, my friend had twisted the focus slightly and given me a new perspective. Some people used their time tending rose gardens. Others smacked balls across grass and sand, aiming for a tiny cup in the ground. What was the point? The prize-winning rose or the hole-in-one? Or the joy of doing it?

I decided "the journey was the destination," and to remind myself of that bit of wisdom, I wrote the words on a yellow sticky and fastened it to my computer. I made up my mind I wasn't going to worry about publication. I was going to learn the craft. Even if my manuscripts ended up in a box, I would turn out the best novels I possibly could.

Once publication became secondary, I felt as if I'd turned on a spigot. The words flowed out. The members of my critique group ooohed and aaahed. I detected a sag in the middle of the manuscript, but I learned more about plot structure at an Oregon Writers Colony workshop at Rockaway, Ore. I got completely caught up in the story and in my characters. Because I wanted them to sound authentic, I mixed and matched the first and last names of my relatives and my high school classmates from Indiana. What difference did it make? The novel wasn't likely to be published anyway.

. . . I wasn't going to worry about publication. I was going to learn the craft.

By then, I could no longer afford the luxury of staying home full-time, so I took a three-day-a-week job at a Seattle agency that handled advertising and marketing for movie studios. Too exhausted to write on the days I worked at the agency, I switched to novelist only on my days off.

I remember saying to my husband, "If I ever do finish this book and sell it, I'll make 17 1/2 cents an hour for the time I put into it." But, even as I complained, I knew I wasn't doing it for the money or the glory. I wrote because it gave me that incomparable creative kick. Despite my frequent declarations to the contrary, I wouldn't have given it up any more than I would have given up on my child.

It took me about eighteen months to write *The Starlite Drive-in*. I should mention that while I told myself that publication wasn't my main goal, I didn't see the harm of trying for it. I pitched the novel at the Pacific Northwest Writers Conference the following summer. When I say I pitched it, I mean I described it to four interested agents in just a few sentences, the way you might summarize the plot of a movie. To my surprise, all four asked me to send them the manuscript.

I chose two agents, careful to note in my letter that I was making a multiple submission. A little warning here: Agents often prefer exclusivity. They don't want to "waste their time" reading your entire manuscript only to find out another agent has beaten them to signing you as a client. I say "too bad." If you have a product that interests more than one agent, let them compete for it. They have no problem rejecting us. However, it's only polite to tell them you're submitting the book to more than one agent.

I was fortunate enough to have both agents offer to represent me. I interviewed them and chose Angela Rinaldi on the basis of her resume and her enthusiasm for my novel. Before starting her own agency, she'd worked as an editor for New York publishers and managed the Los Angeles Times Book Division. Although I was relying on judgment, instinct and luck, the commitment seemed as serious as getting married without the engagement period. I took my chances.

I wrote because it gave me that incomparable creative kick.

Here's how you will know if you made the right choice: Does your agent respond promptly to your telephone calls or e-mail? Does your agent tell you where she's sending your manuscript? Does she follow up by forwarding your rejection letters within a reasonable time? Does she maintain her excitement about your work or does it dwindle with each rejection? (If she really believes in you, she'll reassure you and keep her original enthusiasm.) Is she your advocate (not the editor's or anyone else's)?

If you can't answer yes to these questions, look for a new agent. I know it's difficult to find someone to represent you, but a poor agent won't help. She'll simply delay your progress.

I soon learned Angela was the right one for me. She sold *The Starlite Drive-in* to William Morrow & Company within a few months. Before it even came out in hardcover in July, 1997, it was optioned for film and chosen a *Reader's Digest* Select Edition, a Literary Guild alternate, and a Barnes & Noble Discover Great New Writers selection. It was also picked up by a smattering of foreign countries.

That summer of *Starlite*'s release was a joy. I worked closely with my publicist at Morrow, agreeing to any signing she would arrange for me. The publisher sent me on tour to Indiana and to the West Coast, and I spoke about my writing experience to any newspaper reporter, radio personality, civic organization or book club willing to listen. My critique group threw a party for me and pressured our friends into buying the novel, while I sipped champagne and pretended not to notice.

I had one thousand color postcards printed of the book jacket. I dropped them off at bookstores and sent them to everyone I knew. I paid for the cards, but Morrow offered to pay for the postage (a bigger expense, as it turned out). I dug out the address book from my last high school reunion and mailed postcards to my former classmates. On each card, I wrote a little message that said, in effect, "read this book and see if you're in it." I'm convinced I sold hundreds of copies that way.

> *I dug out the address book from my last high school reunion and mailed postcards to my former classmates.*

On top of my early success with *Starlite*, Morrow offered me a contract for two more novels. I know there are writers who amass story ideas like a squirrel collects nuts, but I'm not one of them. Although I had only the sketchiest idea for a second novel, I seemed to be the only one concerned about that. I signed the contract shortly after *The Starlite Drive-in* was released. The publisher gave me a tidy advance that would allow me to quit my job and live comfortably for a time — while the clock ticked inexorably on my second book.

I punched away at a few story possibilities. I couldn't get excited about them. I couldn't even remember how I came up with the idea for *Starlite*. I missed the characters in that book. I suffered from separation anxiety. I was supposed to be happy about the two-book contract, but after a few frustrating months I wanted to give the advance money back.

"Give the money back?" my husband yelled. "Are you crazy?"

Yes, I thought, I was getting there. I had never intended to become a career novelist. I just wanted to learn how to do it. I wanted to prove I could win first prize in the rose show, smack that hole-in-one. I didn't have a goal beyond that, and I didn't like the way people were already asking, "So, how's your next book coming?"

I came up with a fuzzy story idea about an arson fire in a small town on Washington state's Olympic Peninsula. I tried it out on my writer colleagues.

"Sounds interesting," some said, trying to be supportive.

Others shot it down immediately. "What you should write about is this. . . ." But their suggestions turned out to be their stories, not mine.

Confusion set in. I couldn't even remember how to go about telling a story. I wrote a few scenes, trying to make contact with the characters. I didn't really like them. The heroine was too bitchy. The mother was worse. Why would anyone want to read about these people? Why would anyone want to write about them, for that matter?

"I think you need to soften them a bit," my writer friend Cindy said, tactfully.

"Sounds interesting,"

some said, trying

to be supportive.

I wrote and rewrote. I spun my wheels. I went to sleep thinking about that stupid story, and I woke up thinking about it. I was mired in mud.

Meanwhile, the clock was banging like a jackhammer, and my agent was asking, "How's the book coming?"

Luckily, my editor had forgotten I existed.

And, then, came the dreaded writer's block. Paralysis. One word per hour. At the end of the day, a paragraph of the worst prose you can imagine. A story that went nowhere and interested no one, not even me.

I whined. I felt sorry for myself. I went to New York City to a Literary Guild party in the Starlite Room atop the Waldorf Astoria and pretended I was an author. I read books like *Art and Fear* and *Surviving a Writer's Life*. I tried to work the problem through, logically rather than emotionally. I knew I was dealing with fear, pure and simple fear, but I didn't know how to break through it, how to recover the joy I had once found in writing fiction.

Once again, I made the decision to give up the dream of success. So what if I failed at this second book. It wouldn't be the worst thing that had ever happened to me. I knew in my heart that the Olympic Peninsula story was a good one. So, write the damned book and have a good time doing it, I told myself. I clipped out a little aphorism from a magazine, "don't look at your feet while dancing," and taped it to my computer.

The first draft was awful, but the second one was better. And the third draft was very good, if I do say so myself. I finished the editing on *The Civil Wars of Jonah Moran*, sent off the final manuscript to my editor and immediately began suffering separation anxiety. It's scheduled for publication in six months.

The pressure is on for my third book. The contract says it's due in nine months (childbirth all over again), unless I ask for an extension. But I have this idea. It's about four women friends who commit a tiny, altruistic crime. I can see most of it in my head.

So, what do you think? Sounds like a good story idea, doesn't it?

A Seattle, Wash., native and author of The Starlite Drive-in, *Marjorie Reynolds recently completed her third novel. She is a frequent speaker and workshop leader at writing conferences across the country.*

The Mystery Novel
For Those Working To Write Their First

By Larry Karp

A mystery is a story involving a secret or obscure event, especially a crime, that excites curiosity, and the gradual discovery of who committed it. Here are a few of the many ways writers tell mystery stories, but keep in mind: categories often blend as plots thicken.

In *police procedurals*, cops systematically track down bad guys. *Professional private eyes* are less bound by rules and regulations. Stories in both these forms are usually *hardboiled*, with characters mean as the streets, and a hero more or less reluctantly doing what has to be done. Lots of blood, gallons of hootch, piles of drugs, heavy sex, and torture to taste.

The *amateur detective*, a fellow or gal with an odd predilection for stumbling over murder victims, frequently possesses a specialized field of knowledge and a quick, discerning wit. Some amateur detective stories are hardboiled but, much more often, details of murders are downplayed (or the killings occur offstage), sexual encounters are more genteel, and though there are fist fights and the occasional head conk, mayhem usually is not featured. In the extreme, the story becomes a *cozy*: amateur detective, specified circle of friends, circumscribed environment, no gratuitous violence or sex.

The *caper* is a lighthearted story in which a mastermind puts together an eccentric, even bizarre, scheme involving theft, con games, and/or murder. Much of the mystery centers on the question: will he or she get away with it?

In *romantic suspense*, a spunky, determined heroine (who may tend to seek out danger) dances through a minefield of potential disasters both physical and emotional to finally solve a dastardly crime and fall into the arms of Mr. Right.

Murder is not supposed to be funny but most murder mysteries, hardboileds included, contain humor, black as it sometimes may be. If that bothers you, consider this: who laughs more, St. Peter or Lucifer?

What can I say that might help you write your mystery novel? Here's some of what works and doesn't work for me.

Start with persistence and determination. For a quarter-century I had a job demanding intense concentration, day and night, and with only sporadic fertilization and watering, my poor attempts at book-length fiction withered and died. So I wrote shorter material, mostly nonfiction . . . and the day after I escaped from my distracting profession I began the story that became *The Music Box Murders*. And guess what. The job that had sidetracked me all those years, and the hobby I'd picked up along the way to maintain some degree of sanity now furnished me wonderful plots, settings and characters for my fiction. Those years were not wasted. Keep faith. Keep writing.

I wanted to write mysteries so I read mysteries, a ton of them.

I wanted to write mysteries so I read mysteries, a ton of them. I sampled different forms, asked myself why I liked certain authors and disliked others. I examined the way writers such as Colin Dexter, Lawrence Block, P. D. James, Caroline Graham, Patricia Highsmith, L. R. Wright, Jeremiah Healy and Donald Westlake developed plots and portrayed characters. Listening to dialogue in the books of Elmore Leonard and Ed McBain was a revelation.

But moderation in all things, and proper priorities. A woman recently asked me whether I'd rather write my own book or read someone else's. "I don't read 'til I get my writing done for the day," I said, "and if I don't get to read that particular day, too bad." The woman sighed and nodded. "Yeah. I think that's why I can't get *my* book done. I'd really rather read." Nothing at all wrong with that — I *like* readers. But if I don't write my books, no one will do it for me.

I write what I know; I write what I *love*. Faking it in print's harder to get away with than faking it on the job or in bed. If I don't know what I'm writing about, my factual inaccuracies will stand out like an area of peeling veneer on a woodworking project. Worse, if I don't love what I write, my reader will surely hear my yawns, and you know how contagious yawns are.

How about writing what you hate? Not in fiction, I think. Novels written out of anger, resentment and contempt all too often come off as propaganda, plot set aside as characters stand forlornly, awaiting their next obligation to further the polemic. I can always find something about my bad guys that makes me smile — if sometimes reluctantly.

I write out of my own experience. Not that I *write* my own experience; I write *out* of it. Literally. Putting my own life, even thinly disguised, directly onto paper would drastically limit the imaginative development of my story; better to find an interesting real-life kernel, use it as a jumping-off place, and write *out of it*. Make it all up. That's fun. It's also what fiction is about: trying to uncover and show readers a truth that's been concealed by reality.

Same with characters. I do not try to lift people directly from life: they're already grown and developed. My characters evolve in *their* world, inside my head, and I see and hear them as originals, real people in their own right. Just as I don't know everything about anyone in my real-life, I don't know everything about my

> *I actually felt depressed at the sight of his body. . . .*

characters — but spending time with them, day in and day out, I learn more and more. A few years ago, as I was driving along Interstate 94 in North Dakota, I saw a sign, Exit 238, CLEVELAND GACKLE. This meant the town of Cleveland was just off the highway to the left, and Gackle was 19 miles down the road, but I wasn't thinking about that. I was thinking, what does Cleveland Gackle *look* like? How does he talk? By the time I needed a lockpicker in *Scamming the Birdman*, Cleveland Gackle was rested and ready.

How do I decide who dies in my books? I listen to the story. Harry Hardwick was supposed to be a major character in *The Music Box Murders*, but his insistence that he die on Page One made that problematic. Another character on whom I was counting for long-term service got iced in Chapter Nine. I actually felt depressed at the sight of his body, and rewrote the lead-in to that part of the book three times before I gave up and let the poor man die. That's life. That's fiction. When I saw the same thing coming to another valued character in *Scamming the Birdman*, I just sighed and watched it happen. In the same book, I looked on in horror as evil Vincent LoPriore strangled an old lady's cat; I hadn't even realized the cat was in the room. Nothing I could do about it. Better the cat should go than LoPriore should feel I lacked respect for him.

In portraying honest characters, I think no one tops Ed McBain. I could choke on the politically-correct sensitivity syrup that pours from the mouths of some current mystery heroes, but McBain's detective Steve Carella just goes about his business in the 87th Precinct, *showing himself* to be as compassionate and fair-minded as he is tough, the very model of what a cop should be.

Dialogue's important in carrying a story along; stilted or inconsistent speech is . . . well, murder. When a tough cop, interrogating a suspect, says, "I believe you're reluctant to admit you were in the Rainbow Lounge last Thursday between eight and nine p.m. for fear I will uncover your illicit *affaire de coeur*," I'm through. Next book, please. Not only do I talk to my characters every day, I *listen* to them. Then when it's their turn to speak on a page, I hear their voices clearly. And when I rewrite — sometimes speaking the dialogue aloud — those voices are even clearer: each character edits his or her speech right along with me.

Concentrate fully on writing the book; make it as good as possible.

When my first book was accepted for publication, I found someone else to listen to: my editor. Some of the cuts and changes she recommended in *The Music Box Murders* horrified me — but computers make it so easy to cut and paste, I put them into effect, re-read the text . . . and saw instantly that most were absolutely right. What's more, reviewer comments have unfailingly validated my editor's judgement. Smart writers listen to their editors.

What about selling a first book? For a couple of reasons, I think a writer shouldn't even consider that until the book is written. Marketing's tough, time-consuming and distracting. Concentrate fully on writing the book; make it as good as possible. Then there's actually something to sell. Though a writer may peddle a nonfiction book on the basis of an idea, an outline and a sample chapter or three, most agents and editors want to see the entire manuscript for a first novel. Wouldn't you, if you were in their place?

And if someone does buy a first novel in advance of its completion, this could easily be a curse rather than a blessing. I'm grateful I did not sell *The Music Box Murders* six months after I began writing it; I worked nearly three years, full-time, on that book, and when I was done, it (fortunately) bore little resemblance to what I'd initially envisioned. I was learning as I went, and with no time or structure constraints I was free to wander along to wherever the story was taking me.

Prepublication marketing is a crapshoot with odds high against you, but you can roll a seven only if you play the game. Be persistent, but be professional. Query houses that publish work similar to yours; these days simultaneous submissions are generally accepted, so bring out the shotgun. Go to writers' conventions and conferences: meet editors and agents, talk to published writers. If you have any IOUs, call them in. Be not too proud to be published.

Now drops the other shoe. While you're trying to sell your first book, *don't stop writing*. Work on your second book. Then, when the first one sells, the second will be almost ready for a nice, bang-bang follow up. Or maybe the second will sell and bring along the first. Every finished book shifts odds in your favor, and it's a lot faster to edit books into shape than to write them from scratch . . . and then have to edit them.

How about self-publishing? This doesn't carry the onus it once did, but face it: bookstores won't readily buy from authors, and reviewers still ask whether this is a "vanity press" publication. In any case, selling and distribution are not my thing, but if you've got thick skin, lots of time and a basement with plenty of storage room, you might give it a try. If not, go back to Plan A.

Once my first novel appeared between covers, I came face to face with another aspect of marketing. If I didn't promote my book, it wasn't going to sell . . . and my publisher, logically enough, would not be inclined to bring out more of my mysteries. Like it or not, authors need to go out there, usually on their own nickels; that's just the way it is. I speak on panels and present workshops at mystery fan conventions. I go to libraries; I give readings at bookstores, especially mystery bookshops. Keep in mind: the folks who own mystery bookshops work long hours for very little money because they love mysteries. They *want* authors to appear, because this helps them sell books — especially those of their presenting authors. You're crazy not to want to help them help you.

Support for a writer? Start with the nearest mirror. Writing's a solitary pursuit, but it provides its own consolations. The longer I write, and the more regularly, the better I get to know my characters — and you'd better believe they're going to encourage me. They only exist when I'm thinking about them.

My family and close friends are supportive, pleased when my writing's going well, patting my back or kicking my hiney as indicated when it's not. That's nice. Too many nonwriters seem to regard writing as an amusing little pastime, something writers do occasionally when the spirit moves them; these people can be more than a little irritating. I've often had to choose between a particular social activity and writing; I've occasionally had to choose between writing and a friendship. I've always chosen writing. I've never regretted the choice.

He went through the first chapter as if with a weed whacker, taking out every unnecessary word, phrase, sentence, paragraph, scene.

What about writers' groups? Not for me. To face a weekly censor, well-intentioned though he or she might be, would be a major inhibition to the free flow of my words and ideas. Furthermore, what comes out of my head is *my* story, *my* vision; to permit someone else to tamper with its evolution is to risk disfigurement, even destruction. I don't know who said, "I write to see what I think and believe," but I believe *that*. Only when I've got my story told as well as I can tell it do I ever seek help — and then only from experienced writers or readers.

This has helped me enormously. When I finished *The Music Box Murders*, I showed the manuscript to a novelist-friend, who insisted the book was good and should be published, but only after intensive line-editing. He went through the first chapter as if with a weed whacker, taking out every unnecessary word, phrase, sentence, paragraph, scene. The effect was like tightening screws on a noisy machine: for the first time I heard my own narrative voice — so clearly that I was able to line-edit the rest of the book myself. A few months later — thanks to a strong recommendation from my friend to an editor — I was a soon-to-be-published writer.

What if you just can't figure out how to get your mystery novel started and under way? You've sat, you've written . . . but not much happens. Consider writing classes, taught by competent people. Check with your local university or community college. A good writing teacher can get a beginner organized and moving — but it's like learning to ride a bike. After a certain point if Dad's still running at your side, something's wrong. I'd say once you've gone through three classes, beginner, intermediate, advanced, you ought to be on your own. But should specific problems arise, most writing instructors are glad to make private arrangements with former pupils.

Many mystery bookstores sponsor reading clubs which meet monthly, and these provide fine learning opportunities through the discussion of good and bad points of books by writers other than yourself. Check out Seattle's Mystery Bookstore and Portland's Murder By The Book.

Mystery conventions offer more than panels and workshops — there's the chance to talk informally to other writers, editors, agents and fans. I've particularly enjoyed Left Coast Crime (www.LeftCoast Crime), Malice Domestic (www.erols.com/malice) and Bouchercon (www.bouchercon2001.com).

If the internet's your thing, go to Mysterious Strand (www.idson-line.com/user-web/cwilson/mystery.htm) and Sisters In Crime (www.books.com/sinc/links); these sites provide links to major mystery and mystery writer sites. To access mystery discussion groups, try www.alecwest.com/mysvault.htm.

Aspiring writers have ambition; that's almost a given. Most have at least a fair share of talent; otherwise they'd find writing painful and do something else with their time. In the end, success usually comes down to discipline and persistence. If you want to be a writer, *be* a writer. It's a great life. Go for it!

Larry Karp, who lives in Seattle, Wash., was a practicing physician for close to twenty-five years. During that time he wrote continuously. His works include numerous magazine and newspaper articles, as well as three nonfiction books about the worlds of medicine and music boxes. His mysteries include: The Music Box Murders, The Midnight Special, Scamming the Birdman *and* The Sorcerer and the Junkman.

Writing and Marketing *Cold Oceans*

By Jon Turk

Phase I: Writing the Book

About twenty-five years ago I was eating dinner with some friends in La Conner, Wash. A young man walked in and someone said, "Hi, Tom; meet Jon Turk, he's a writer, like you."

Tom looked at me and asked, "What kind of stuff do you write?"

"Science textbooks."

He shrugged as if to dismiss me, "Well, I write insanity textbooks." I soon learned that 'Tom' was Tom Robbins and he had just released his first book, *Another Roadside Attraction*.

I had been trained as a chemist and had started writing environmental science texts in 1970. The books were successful but now, four years and three books later, I wanted to write for a broader audience. I read Tom's book and tried to imagine writing something like it. No way! My mind didn't revolve in those circles.

Starting with the basics, I mentally separated writing into two components, the clarity of expression and the message. Textbooks trained me to explain complex issues clearly, but I had no idea what I wanted to say. I spent time with Tom and watched him in casual moments. His innate personality had the same zany, loony, off-the-wall style that he projected in his books. So the first lesson, which should have been obvious from the start, was to be myself. Then I had a scary thought, "Was it enough to be myself? Was I interesting enough?"

I tried to think of a plot for a novel, but failed. What about nonfiction? Well, I enjoyed canoeing and rock climbing, maybe I could try an adventure story. Nothing happened.

Five years later, I tried to kayak around Cape Horn but shipwrecked off a lonely coastline in the Antarctic Ocean. A few years after that, I attempted to row across the Northwest Passage, but encountered impassible ice and stopped woefully far from my goal. The next year I tried to dogsled up the coast of Baffin Island in winter, but my partner and I quarreled and the expedition dissolved on a wind swept frozen ocean.

My textbooks were orderly and controlled, but the rest of my life was filled with disaster. I had never read a book with the theme: "I tried

50

to climb a mountain and didn't get to the top and then I tried to climb another mountain and didn't get to the top of that one either, and so on." But I sensed that if I was going to become a writer, this was my milieu. So I started. When I thought that I had produced a polished chapter, I took a one-week writing seminar from Peter Matthiessen. He read my manuscript and told me that I had the skeleton of a publishable story, but first I had to learn how to write.

That comment was disconcerting because by this time I had written nine books with combined sales of a quarter of a million copies. But then I realized that I had to add a third element to the essence good writing, the lyrical cadence of the prose. A textbook style wouldn't do. I plugged away, working in isolation, trying to lift each scene from the mundane to the magical. During the next decade, I became detached from the concept that I was actually working for money and just kept writing because that is the kind of person that I am.

. . . I became detached from the concept that I was actually working for money and just kept writing. . . .

Gradually, I realized that I was writing about my life at the same time that I was living it, so the plot kept unfolding and the theme matured. I succeeded in paddling from Ellesmere Island to Greenland and worked that story into the chronicle of past failures. Finally, I "finished" the manuscript, wrapped it with protective cardboard, snapped a rubber band around it and set it on the edge of my desk.

A friend gave me the name of an agent in San Francisco so I sent her the book. A month went by; two months; three months; four and no word. I followed up with a careful note asking her if she had found time to read my work. The agent quickly reminded me that she was an important person in a big city and that I was a lowly writer wanna-be from a hick town in the woods and that she didn't have time to do me a favor, which would most probably be unprofitable for her. Because I had shown such arrogance in sending a follow-up note, she decided to reject the book without reading it. Furthermore, she intended to throw the manuscript in the garbage without deigning to return it in the stamped, self-addressed envelope I had provided.

WHEW!

If this was the writing world, I wanted no part of it. But after a few years I regained courage and sent the manuscript to an agent in New York. Throughout our relationship, he has shown me kindness and patience, reaffirming my belief that everyone has a basic human right to respect. Acceptance by an agent is only a beginning and we soon faced a sequence of rejections by publishers. Gradually, I saw patterns in the criticisms, and decided to rework the manuscript one more time.

On January 27, 1997, I was caught in an avalanche in British Columbia. As I wrote in *Cold Oceans,*

> The next day, after the surgeons had bolted my pelvis back together, I lay on my hospital bed, dazed on morphine, staring at all those tubes transporting fluids into and out of my body. My roommate was watching television. I pushed the call button and asked the nurse to close the curtains. I knew that Oprah wasn't my salvation. When I returned home, Chris rented a small hydraulic crane from a hospital supply company. Every morning for the following six weeks, Chris jacked me out of bed, lowered me into a Lazy-boy recliner and spread all the necessities around my chair — lunch, a few cookies, a water bottle, a telephone, a book and a laptop computer. Then she put on her parka and left to ski powder. I always ate my cookies as soon as the door closed. Munching slowly, I traveled back across the remote landscapes, trying to understand where my journeys had led me and where they would take me as soon as I could walk again.

It's a funny twist of fate that a personal tragedy gave me the final boost to finish the book. However, my writing persona had become wrapped around my normal life symbiotically, exchanging strength and weakness until the two became mutually dependent on one another.

Part II: The Contract

In April, I received two offers, one from a small press and one from HarperCollins. A few months previously, *The New Yorker* had run an article claiming that large publishing companies had lost an appreciation for literature and were driven instead by "bottom line CEO's" hungry to sign famous celebrities and to return sure bets for their stockholders. A first time author could be lost in the brouhaha and have his or her book ignored. New York seemed like a scary world.

Initially, I thought that I should sign with the small company even though they offered me a considerably smaller advance. Before I made my decision, I called the owner of my local bookstore and asked him to assume that he didn't know me. Would he be more likely to stock and display *Cold Oceans* if it was published by HarperCollins or by a small press? Without hesitation he said, "HarperCollins." I picked up the phone and called my agent.

Phase III: New York

The production details proceeded smoothly through jacket design, copyediting and proofs. The activity quieted down while the book went to the printer, so I decided to go on a ski expedition. On the outbound flight I stopped in New York to visit my new editor, Megan Newman. (As an aside, even though publishers won't buy you a ticket to New York, I recommend footing the bill just to personalize the relationship.) The conversation was warm and friendly. I didn't feel that I was working for a large company; I felt that I was working with a person who had supported my book, liked it and believed in it.

Then we went upstairs to talk to one of the money czars. He asked me to discuss possible book tour plans and I outlined an extended route from my home in Darby, Mont., to Seattle, south to San Diego, across to Denver and then looping back to Darby. The czar nodded and then told me, "You realize that we don't have the budget to support such an ambitious project."

I turned and said, "I've worked on this book for a third of my life; if it is successful, someone will publish my next book, if it fails, my dream will be badly shaken. I'm an adventure travel writer; I can live cheaply out of the back of my pick-up. I'm doing the tour." I paused, "Maybe you could pick up a Motel 6 once a week just so I could take a shower."

The czar shook his head no.

"How about a grand slam sausage and egg breakfast at Denny's every Sunday morning?"

No one thought I was funny.

"OK," I said. "I'm going anyway."

Phase IV: The Tour

On the road, late at night, fighting fatigue, I concentrated on the confluence of the white and the dotted lines in my headlights. My publicist could not comprehend distances in the west. This time, she booked me an evening reading in a store in Montrose, Colo., followed by a 7:00 AM radio interview in Colorado Springs, 235 miles away. Dark spruce shadowed the roadside as I drove over the continental divide, and then I descended to the semiarid plain below. I slept a few hours in a ditch, followed the incipient sunrise east, brushed my teeth and washed my face at a roadside eatery, and made it to the radio station with half an hour to spare.

Waiting in the hallway, I quietly practiced answering expected questions in an animated radio voice. A road weary, all-night-drive presentation wouldn't do. I entered the studio during the newscast, adjusted the mike, put on the headphones and chatted briefly off the air with the interviewer.

Publication of *Cold Oceans,* the culmination of my dream and perhaps the greatest professional success of my life, had vaulted me to the level of the urban homeless, living alone on bad food, little sleep, and a seemingly endless tunnel of bookstores, studios, and fake living rooms in front of television cameras.

An average bookstore has between 10,000 and 100,000 titles. Beyond my circle of friends, no one knew my name or had any reason to choose my book from the multitude. So I was working the trenches, hoping that people would walk into a store and think, "I heard that guy, Jon Turk; he was pretty interesting; I think I'll buy *Cold Oceans.*"

The strategy was working. I paid off my advance and everyone was making a small profit. HarperCollins had even found the money to reimburse me for my travel expenses. I quit writing textbooks and started thinking about the next book.

John Turk, chemist by training and an adventurer by avocation, has written numerous environmental and Earth Science textbooks, as well as articles for several publications. He lives with his wife and expedition partners in Darby, Mont., and in the Kootenay Mountains of British Columbia. His most recent adventure was completing a small boat expedition across the North Pacific Rim from Japan to Alaska.

Freelancing: One Man's Meat
(with apologies to E.B. White)
By Doug Rennie

In 1991, I finished my 27th year of teaching and decided that, when I hit 70, I didn't want to look back and think: You did one thing your whole life. So I quit the classroom, moved with my wife to Portland, and morphed into a freelance writer.

Well, like Hogan's knuckleheaded nemesis Sergeant Schultz, I knew nothing — NUUUUTTTHINK! — about how to go about this. So I ambled down to Powell's Bookstore and bought some "How To" books on freelancing (one promised me $85K a year if I but did things his — her? I forget — way). I brought them home and scanned them and — voila — there it was, laid out in a dozen crisp little can't miss-chapters: The Secret.

I remember puppy-wiggling all over and feeling giggling-level giddy at how simple it all seemed.

First, see, you get this really neat idea, then you concoct a seductive little story synopsis (these chapters invariably contain words like "hook" and "grabber") which you include in something called a "query letter."

Then it gets even easier: Clip on a SASE, mail your query in and wait for the contract to arrive in, oh, a few weeks, say. A month at the outside. And for God's sake, never, never send out the same query letter to more than one publication at a time. Because, boy, just how screwed are you going to be when BOTH *The New Yorker* and *The Atlantic Monthly* send you contracts?

The Horror! The Horror!

Nope. You send your pitch to one publication period, and only IF they send back a rejection (hey, it's possible!) do you submit to another. To do otherwise is called "simultaneously submitting" — an unthinkable, even odious practice accorded the status and stench of an overflowing commode.

So that's what I did. Read the books. Learned The Secret. Followed the Formula.

For nearly three months, I thought up cool ideas, spelled them out in beguiling query letters and fired them off all over the country — making certain I logged each in my submissions log.

Then I waited for my SASEs to come home.

And waited some more.

I don't remember what it was — two months, three — that the rejections began to dribble in, generally a half sheet upon which was printed "Not Right for Us" or "Doesn't Meet Our Needs at the Present Time" or "Can't Use This. Sorry." About every third SASE contained my tri-folded query letter and nothing more, suggesting the manure I'd sent wasn't worth wasting a form rejection on. Some SASEs I never got back; and I still haven't eight years later.

I never saw my SASE again. Instead, I got a phone call. . . .

In the interim, exploiting my background as a lifelong competitive athlete and marathon runner, I did manage to land regular assignments in Portland's *Willamette Week*'s then new "Head to Toe" section. The first thing I wrote for WW — and my first published work as a free-lancer — was in January, 1992: a 2,500-word story on IQ-boosting pharmaceuticals called "Smart Drugs."

A few days after the story appeared, I was running on the Wildwood Trail when I was struck by one of those lightning bolt epiphanies: Why not send this same cutting-edge story (little had been printed on Smart Drugs at the time) to some national magazine? So I did. I typed up a letter that began not with a query, but with the words "Enclosed for your consideration. . ." and clipped it to a hard copy of the "Smart Drugs" story. Then I mailed it to *Men's Fitness*.

I never saw my SASE again. Instead, I got a phone call maybe two weeks later. It was the magazine's managing editor. They'd take the story and pay me $600. They wanted to use it right away, he said, and told me to send them an invoice, that there wasn't time for the usual contract procedure. A fresh-faced novice, I didn't know what an invoice was. "A bill," he said. "Just send in the title of the story and the amount: $600, and we'll mail you a check within a week or so after we get it." So I did. The check arrived ten days later.

This event was the El Alamein, the midway of my freelance career. THE turning point. From now on, instead of heeding the behest of the

How To pundits, I would heed Sinatra and do it My Way.

And I have. For going on eight years now. In that time I've had (near as I can figure) 35 short stories and around 500 articles, features, stories, op-ed pieces, columns, essays and reviews published in newspapers, journals and magazines — local, regional, national. I've been paid as little as author complimentary copies and as much as $2,500. I've also had a lot of stuff — a lot — rejected. Unless you're Joan Didion or John Updike, there's no way around that.

In my less than a decade as a trial-and-error freelancer, there are some things that I've found work better than others in getting published. A lot of them run counter to that, ah, conventional wisdom. So feel free to gasp in outrage, cluck your tongue disapprovingly, shake your head, make faces, shriek "This guy doesn't know his ass!!!!" as you hurl your *Northwest Writers Handbook* against the wall — and reject any or all of the following tips.

All I'm saying here, all I mean to say, is that these practices have worked better for me — by far — than the pat formulas in the How To books.

So, here goes.

Don't waste your time on query letters. Otherwise, you'll spend all your writing time cranking out the damn things. If you have a good (perhaps great) idea, write the story. Then find a market for it. If it's a strong story, it will find a home.

I have never sold a single piece — literally, not one — through a query letter. Every sale has been the result of sending either a complete manuscript or, lacking that, the first 2-5 pages of a story in progress, enough to allow an editor to see its shape and style. This is especially important for beginning writers who have few, if any, published clips to send along with the query letters. Editors are under pressure every week, month, whatever to feed the beast, and they're just not going to assign a story to an inexperienced writer (unless he/she writes one hell of a query, preferably one that purports to have proof that Di was really killed by the CIA to cover-up her affair with Alan Greenspan).

But if they have the story right there in front of them and that first paragraph is a "grabber" (sorry, couldn't help myself). . . .

Carpet bomb the bastards. Flat out ignore this "one submission to one publication at a time" crap. You can wait three or four months easy for your SASE to come home, more often than not bearing a rejection. Six months isn't uncommon. Neither is no response — ever. You can turn into mummy dust waiting for some editors to reply.

So, unless a publication explicitly prohibits simultaneous submissions (surprisingly, not that many do), send out your cover letter and story to half a dozen publications at a time — more even if the potential markets are there. The odds of more than one acceptance are minuscule, and even if this does occur, many magazines or newspapers have no problem with the same story appearing elsewhere as long as it's not a rival in the same geographical area.

. . . Focus on mid-level magazines, both regional . . . and national. . . .

Go "off Broadway." You could win the Oregon Lottery. You could. And you might get something accepted at *Harper's*, *Vanity Fair*, or *Rolling Stone*. The odds are about the same. But for writers like us, it's pretty much a waste of time, paper and postage to send stuff to the high-rent pubs. Instead, focus on mid-level magazines, both regional (you don't always have to live in and/or write about "their" area; honest) and national; those that pay between, say, $200 and $500-$800 for a feature-length piece. Dream all you want, but when you consider markets, be realistic, too.

And speaking of markets: Stick to *Writer's Market* and you'll compete for the same spaces as every other freelancer from Medford to Maine; Now, *WM* is fine. We all use it. But for thousands of paying markets everyone else doesn't submit to, thumb through *The National Directory of Magazines* (most libraries carry it).

Writer's Market lists 1,750 magazine markets; *NDM* lists 20,000 — most of which you've never seen or heard of; everything from the quasi-normal (*Mothering*) to the borderline bizarre (*Hip Mama*). Most of these markets pay, some pretty well. Many of my earliest sales — *Trip & Tour, Book Lover, Futurific, Mountain Living, Down Memory Lane*, among others — were to periodicals not found in *Writer's Market*.

Go short. It's easier to sell shorter pieces — say, 500 to 1,000 words — than it is longer ones. Keep this in mind when you're thinking up story ideas. Many magazines and/or newspapers have a bunch of slots (rotating columns, one page end paper pieces, fillers, single item hot news kinds things, etc.) for short stuff, but far fewer for full-length features, many of which are contracted to established writers with lengthy and impressive publication credits (and if you're one of them, you shouldn't read this).

Chunky-style sells. There's a trend in publishing these days (particularly in mainstream magazines) called "chunking:" breaking a story up into small-to-medium sized "chunks" or sidebars that can be then arranged on the page in an eye-catching array of columns, graphs, pie charts, squares, rectangles, triangles and trapezoids. The printed word for the MTV generation. *Runner's World* magazine, for whom I write regularly, has already informed me to start turning in my copy chunk friendly. Like it or not, that's where the reading — and writing — life is headed in the New Millennium. So it seems to me that, in general, the conventional 2,000-word story has less chance of acceptance than an 800-world core story to hang everything on with what's left divided up into a trio or quartet of discreet chunks.

Learn to love lists. The closest you're going to come to a guaranteed sale is a hooky lead paragraph and clever conclusion wrapped around some "Best Of" or "Top Ten (Five, Eight, whatever) list, each item described in a few (to a half dozen) vivid sentences. It's called the Service Piece: "Eight Reasons Why Men Cheat;" "Ten Little Known Tax Saving Tips;" "Five Great Spa Weekends;" "Ten Best Oregon Coast Bookstores/Past Places/Burger Joints/Art Galleries/Budget Resorts/ Handicapped Hiking Trails/You Get the Idea" (write these and *The Oregonian's A&E* will buy). Newspapers and periodicals both regional and national lust after such stories — which, of course, are also exemplary chunking candidates.

Has it occurred to you yet that (ten tips; count 'em) you're now about halfway through such a story?

Recycle. When you sell a piece, *immediately* think about where you can sell it next. It makes no sense — none — to spend all that time writing a saleable story then put it in the closet after someone buys it. Instead, re-sell that sucker. then re-sell it again. And again. My Father's Day essay, "A Good Man," has been published (for decent cash) four times (so far). And it's still got legs. I plan to milk this baby for another ten years. If you do holiday-pegged stuff, send it out every year — and a good four to six months early. And just think how many markets there are for those high-demand "list" pieces.

Drop down the food chain. I don't have hard numbers, but I know I've sold more stories when I've mailed them NOT to the Editor/Editor-in-chief, but instead to some Assistant or Associate Editor a few pegs down on the masthead. You have to actually get a copy of the mag to get these names because you won't find them in the *Writer's Market* listings. I don't know why this works, but it seems to. I have never received anything other than a form rejection from *Harper's* or the *The Atlantic Monthly*, for example, when I addressed my submission to the Trail Boss; but I have gotten back nice personal notes (at the bottom of a form rejection, of course) from *Harper's* (twice) and *The Atlantic Monthly* (three times) when I submitted to one of the mid-level wranglers. In every case, the substance of the hand-penned note suggested that someone actually read what I sent.

And isn't this the lot of the freelancer? I mean, think about it: In what other endeavor would a rejection of your efforts — simply because it was handwritten — make you feel so good?

Market day. You're not just a writer, you're also a businessperson Which means you need to sell your stuff. Which means mailing it out. Regularly. Set aside one day (or afternoon/evening/whatever you can) a week *solely* for assembling and mailing submission packets. No one is going to break into your house, steal your manuscripts, sell them to magazines and send you checks. You have to do this grunt work yourself. And you have to do it *every week*. There is no other way. Don't get bummed out by rejections, either; you're like every other salesman out there pimping his/her wares. Some marks buy, most don't. Live with it.

That's it. Those are my Ten Tips for 2003. Direct your hostile phone calls, email rants and threatening letters directly to this publication, not to my home.

Doug Rennie, a Portland, Ore. writer, whose essays and stories have appeared in nearly 100 periodicals, literary journals, and anthologies, is also a marathon runner, bicyclist and traveler. His first collection of stories and essays, Badlands, *was recently published and he is currently working on a novel,* One Cool Cat.

In Pursuit of Poetry

By David Hedges

Poetry, that poor step-child of the arts — maligned, misunderstood, even feared — is thriving as never before, despite the fact that few poets throughout history have made a living at it. In fact, if you take the time poets spend at what Dylan Thomas described as his "craft or sullen art" and translate it into cents (forget the dollars), the minimum wage looms as an astronomical amount. As Oregon poet Dianne Averill so aptly put it, "Poetry is like crime. It doesn't pay."

"So why," ask those whose sole focus is the Bottom Line, "do poets bother?" Why indeed! Ask a dozen poets and you might hear a dozen variations on the theme, but all write poetry for the same reason bears do what they do in the woods — it's natural.

I'm talking about the basic manifestations of the poetic soul: boundless curiosity . . . a keen sense of the world around . . . something to say . . . a need to be heard.

A poet's engine may be driven by a flickering flame or a raging inferno, but just as surely as when gasoline and oxygen mix and a spark ignites them, there is combustion when observation and realization come together in a poet's mind, and the desire to preserve that image, that insight, that moment, causes words to flow. What poet has not grabbed the first available scrap of paper — a napkin, an envelope, a grocery receipt — to jot down a sudden thought before it escaped? What writer?

This raises an old debate, one with as much chance of resolution as the "chicken vs. egg" conundrum. Are poets simply writers who've picked a particular branch of the writing tree, or do they inhabit a tree of their own? While interviewing William Stafford for the 1991 *Writers Northwest Handbook*, I asked when it was he first thought of himself as a poet. His answer fell to the editor's sword, but it merits resurrection: "I don't think of myself as a poet. I'm a writer. That's what I do."

I go along with that . . . to a point. I'm a writer by virtue of having done nothing else to earn money for the past 40 years, but I consider myself, first and foremost, a poet. It's a state of mind more than a hard-wired fact.

Before my sophomore year in high school, I hated writing assignments with a passion. What's more, I felt I had better things to do than sit around and read books: I had places to explore, discoveries to make, adventures to try. I lifted book reports from *Classic Comics*. Then, on a fateful morning in the fall of 1951, poet Laurence Pratt stepped into a classroom at Lake Oswego Union High School in Portland, said "Good Morning," and began reciting *Beowulf* . . . in Old English! Like Steve Martin in "The Jerk," I'd found my rhythm, my purpose.

Mr. Pratt sent a poem of mine to the National High School Poetry Anthology; it was published with Special Mention. When I graduated, he handed me a copy of his second book, *Harp of Water*, in which he had penned, "To David Hedges, who has shown skill in poetical composition." Whether or not I had any claim to the title, I *was* a poet. *Cogito, ergo sum.*

> *. . . poetry has crept into (almost) everything I've written.*

The poet in me has influenced (almost) every aspect of my life for as long as I can remember. And poetry has crept into (almost) everything I've written.

The Oregonian told me I could start as a copy boy and work my way up to rewriting obituaries. I snapped up a job with the Oregon City *Enterprise-Courier* and found myself covering seven beats. I'd edited the *Beaver dam*, an off-campus humor magazine at Oregon State . . . so, the poet not content with reporting news, I asked if I could write a daily humor column. And I did, nightly, on my own time, for no pay above my $70-a-week salary. Most of the columns played off a snippet of verse, such as Alexander Pope's epigram, "Words are like leaves, and where they most abound, / Much fruit of sense beneath is rarely found." All had a foot firmly planted in Fantasyland.

I called my column "One Man's Poison . . . ," figuring everyone was familiar with the English proverb. I managed to make a poet of at least one reader, the man who labeled me "the bilious boy with the poison pen." Note the poetic devices: the alliteration, the assonance. In 1962, as publications editor at Reed College, Portland, Ore., I graced the cover of *The Sallyport*, the quarterly alumni magazine, with a photo of a young woman in a frilly dress reclining in the crotch of a flowering cherry tree, reading a book. Inside, I waxed poetic over signs of springtime's transformation of the campus, complete with a headline of my own design, a curlicued *Spring!* on every page of the cover story. Howls rose from alumni protesting the un-Reedie-like image on the cover, the original cartoons used to illustrate a scholarly article, and a wide range of other depravities, not the least of which was my *Spring!*

The following year I jumped to First National Bank of Oregon, the state's largest financial institution, as public information director. I took the bimonthly employee magazine, *FNB Statement*, and pumped it full of poetry. In an essay on the company picnic, "A picnic is . . .," I captured the ambiance, the cloudburst, the laughter of children, but failed to mention a single banker by name. Vice presidents and assistant vice presidents scrambled for seats on the Publications Committee, which had never before convened, protesting the un-banker-like look and feel of their magazine. The Tar-and-Feathers Subcommittee was primed for a night ride when a memo came down from the president, saying he liked what I was doing. Saved!

> . . . poets, those odd creatures who wander off the path at every opportunity. . . .

Looking back at my checkerboard career, I can see why those who view life as a straight-line activity — first you're born, then you die — cast jaundiced eyes at poets, those odd creatures who wander off the path at every opportunity, stopping not only to smell the roses, but to ponder, as did England's Monty Python gang, "The Meaning of Life." Those weirdos who undermine the status quo. Those harbingers of social change who rail against injustice. Those keen-eyed seekers after Truth and Beauty. . . . (Years ago, this is where one of my kids would interrupt me with, "Dad, you're lecturing again.")

Pardon the double negative, but I've reached the point where I can't *not* be a poet. Poetry surrounds me, envelops me, permeates me, issues from my pores. I leap at every opportunity to share my hopes and fears, my innermost thoughts and feelings, the views through my windows on the world. But in the immortal words of Peter Sellers, aka Dr. Pratt (no relation to Laurence) in *The Wrong Box*, "I was not always as you see me now." For the first 40 years of my life, I mimed Robert Burns's "wee, sleekit, cow'rin, tim'rous beastie." I was not The Mouse That Roared, but the poet afraid to "squeak up."

A stool stands just fine on three legs, but a poet's chair needs four. Beyond your art and craft, you need to publish, and to read aloud before a room full of strangers. Otherwise, the only outside feedback you'll receive is the sound of one hand clapping. Feedback is like fertilizer to a poet's soul; it enhances growth.

I owe a debt to the late Penny Avila, for years the doyenne of Oregon poetry, who dragged me, kicking and screaming, from my cozy nest. As poetry editor of *The Oregonian's Northwest Magazine*, she asked for, and published, the first poem I'd submitted since high school. She pushed me on-stage for my first reading before a live audience . . . pulled me to my first open mike . . . talked me into reading Dylan Thomas with her on radio. (The engineer said "Thirty seconds." My shirt collar shrank three sizes. My voice went up an octave, and took on a vibrato; everyone said I sounded like Dylan Thomas, though I have no recollection.)

Plopping a cherry atop the sundae, she surprised me at a William Stafford workshop she'd organized: when KGW-TV showed up, and the cameras clicked on, *I* was the poet she picked to read; Stafford spent the entire 20 minutes discussing *my* poem.

You may not have a Penny Avila in your corner, but you can seek out opportunities on your own. Unless you pretend to the throne of Emily Dickinson, hoping your poems will be discovered in an old steamer trunk, you need to publish and perform to be complete as an artist. As Penny used to say, "Believe me, honey, it'll do ya good." Believe me, it did.

Publishing made easy: bundle up several of your best poems, shoot them off to *The New Yorker*, and gleefully anticipate the looks on your poet-friends' faces when you tell them where *your* work will soon appear. Personally, I find the marketing side of poet-biz about as appealing as emptying a day-old diaper pail . . . necessary, but odious.

Bill Stafford talked of his amazement when, back before he was known, *The Hudson Review* accepted several of his poems. Even after he became the most widely published poet in America, he admitted placing only 10 percent of the poems he sent out. His secret (beyond excellence) was to keep his poems constantly circulating, like a juggler with a dozen oranges in the air. This way, you soothe the pain of rejection by shifting your hopes to the remaining poems . . . but at the same time, you toss the "failures" right back into the mix.

In comparing notes with other poets, I've learned of several novel approaches. One poet said she opens *Poet's Market* to a random page, and whatever listing her finger lands on receives the next submission. Another said he prints 'em until he has a nice stack, and once or maybe twice a year, sends 'em out like a flock of pigeons, knowing most will come home to roost. (Both these poets have won prestigious national prizes!)

Yet another haunts Portland's cigar stores, reading every poetry journal on the rack, hoping to find a fit. There is validity to this approach. You learn where your poems stand the least chance of acceptance: no traditional verse to *The American Poetry Review*, unless your name is Richard Wilbur, or free verse to *The Formalist*, unless your name is W. S. Merwin.

But never attempt to second guess the editors of all the other literary periodicals in the land. I sent a syllabic sonnet sequence to *Poet Lore* despite not having seen anything even remotely similar in a previous issue . . . and they took it.

The Yellow Pages Bookstore in Grants Pass, Ore., has accumulated a collection of literary magazines to aid local writers unsure of where to submit what. Bravo! If every town boasted such a repository, in a bookstore or library, writers would be spared all manner of expense, including wear and tear on the psyche. This is the stuff of Ford Foundation grants. Think of the lifeline this would toss to praiseworthy publications struggling to stay afloat!

Dylan Thomas was right: poets exercise their "craft or sullen art" alone, immersed in the workings of their hearts and minds, often while the world sleeps. For this reason, poets, as with all artists, benefit from a sense of community, ties with a wider universe.

Most new poets start by showing their first halting efforts to an intimate, the one person each is reasonably sure will turn a sympathetic ear (won't laugh). Many find clusters of like-minded souls eager to share their work; some stay with their critique groups for decades. In the mid-70s, I was welcomed into the Mt. Hood Poetry Circle, which included Dr. Walter Kidd (aka Conrad Pendleton), Penny Avila, Sister

Helena Brand, Eloise Hamilton (first president of the Verseweavers Poetry Society, predecessor of the Oregon State Poetry Association), Dr. James Stauffer, Ethel Fortner and a host of other local luminaries . . . all passed *ad astra*, gone to Elysian fields.

Some attend readings when noted poets pass through town, or frequent open mike readings, perchance to read, once they muster their courage. Others, especially those isolated by geography (or preference) from the urban and academic poetry scenes, find community at workshops and conferences, or in groups such as the Oregon State Poetry Association, which offers both, plus contests — another stimulus to growth.

Throwing yourself into a well-organized workshop with an able leader is like plugging yourself into an electrical circuit.

By community I mean more than rubbing elbows with workshop leaders, schmoozing with fellow poets, or flashing membership cards. I mean *connecting* . . . with something bigger than yourself, something seated at the center of your being. No matter how active your imagination, how finely honed your skills, you still need, periodically, to recharge your batteries.

Like the psychiatrist who undergoes routine psychoanalysis, I take workshops, as well as lead them. Throwing yourself into a well-organized workshop with an able leader is like plugging yourself into an electrical circuit. Light bulbs pop on. Images appear, fuzzy at first, but increasingly sharp as you pull them into focus. Words find their way to paper. You come away energized — and, on sublime occasions, with altered perceptions.

Such was the case with my first workshop — but getting there was an ordeal. Like a love-struck adolescent in love, clutching a bouquet of poems in a hot fist, heart pounding like a tom-tom gone berserk in my chest, I approached the meeting room at the Multnomah County Library, Portland, Ore., on rubber legs. The workshop leader, Doreen Gandy Wiley, was so welcoming, so *friendly*, I agreed to sacrifice my poem at the altar. . . and allow it to be dissected. She liked it! The others had good things to say. I floated out of there on a cloud, and didn't come down for a week.

Later experiences were mixed. One workshop leader of note looked at my work and muttered, "This is not a poem." At last, a poet across the circle broke the stunned silence by bravely stating, "I think it's a poem." Another workshop leader seemed to fix solely on minutiae, ignoring the poem's theme, its reason for being. Lesson: well-known poets come in all sizes and shapes — mental, emotional and spiritual, as well as physical.

For this reason, it's best to take as many workshops as you have time and money for . . . or none at all. One workshop points your compass in a certain direction; a second shifts it any number of degrees; a third gives you triangulation, a new set of referents. To chart your own course, you need a compass that swings full circle. You reach this point not by taking 360 workshops, but by stowing the good advice — what applies or appeals to you — and pitching the excess baggage overboard.

Conferences offer a number of workshop alternatives, along with readings, lectures and opportunities to share your work. You'll find excellent examples elsewhere in this book. Like the old Buddy Hackett routine, you pick from Column A and Column B until your plate is full. Centrum. Haystack. (I dare not continue.) The names alone trigger veritable floods of memories in the minds of those who've taken part.

But not everyone equates "biggest" with "best." Personally, I prefer the laid-back atmosphere, the lower amps, of Oregon Writers Colony workshops. Though a presenter at the three I attended, I threw myself into a range of activities, and came away feeling I'd been to a well-planned family reunion. Oregon State Poetry Association conferences are similar in that respect: you get out of them what you put in, with no external pressure. *Support* is the name of the game. Beginners and old hands feel equally at home. And the price is right.

A word of caution: avoid stating that you "studied with" or "under" a prominent poet unless you were enrolled in a college or university program for more than a term or semester and had regular face-to-face contact. Nothing flashes "amateur" on your marquee more surely than claiming rights to a workshop or conference poet without saying where. Truth will out.

No one knows where poetry is headed. It's not a free market commodity, like pork belly futures, where buy-sell orders point the way. It's not subject to whims of fashion, though some might argue that slam poetry is a here-today-and-gone-tomorrow phenomenon, and as for rap . . . but that's another issue.

For clues to the future, let's dip into the distant past, to poetry's roots: mnemonic ("how-to") poetry verses to help farmers, for example, remember when to plant and harvest . . . all very practical. Fast forward to the time when kings kept their thrones, and their heads, based on their ability to spout impromptu poetry. To when balladeers, the medieval equivalent of the Internet, entertained the masses while informing the masses' intelligencia of life in the wider world. the great ages of Western civilization, where poets held mirrors to society's face. And finally, to America after World War Two . . . more precisely, after the Beats rose and fell.

As Walt Whitman wrote, "To have great poets, you must have great audiences, too."

Stagnation set in when the clones of near-great poet-teachers spawned a generation whose look-alike, sound-alike paeans to solipsism marched imperiously across the pages of respected journals, and no one trusted the inner voice whispering: "The emperor's as naked as a jay." (There I go, lecturing again.)

Today's poetry is as diffuse, as fragmented, as today's society. There are good poets swimming in the soup, but no great ones have yet bobbed to the surface. The yawn on the face of a populace bombarded daily with messages to last a lifetime speaks to the downsizing of the American brain. In the collective consciousness, poetry is reduced to Spam haiku, and greeting card verse. Yet individual poets are making themselves heard. The "craft or sullen art" appears set for a renaissance.

Presumptuous, perhaps, but not unfounded. As Walt Whitman wrote, "To have great poets, you must have great audiences, too." And despite the pressures of modern life — or (radical thought) because of those pressures — the audience for poetry is growing. As more people look to the contemplative arts for relief from chaos and cacophony, the best new poets in the land will draw increasing numbers. If 700 Portlanders will spend $10 to hear Adrienne Rich, what next?

As president of OSPA, I'm keenly aware of poetry's resurgence in Oregon. In two years, I've seen our membership increase 350 percent (112 to 393), conference registrations triple, contest entries quadruple. In 1999, the first statewide Oregon Student Poetry Contest drew 1,011 entries from every corner of the state. Parents, grandparents, teachers, students and other well-wishers filled every nook and cranny of the hall at Lane Community College to hear the young people read their winning poems.

Penetrating the sometimes thick barriers placed in its path, poetry has at last reentered the mainstream of American life. There is recognition that whistles and bells are no substitute for the sound of the wind. That the eyes sometimes see more when they're closed. That the ears are funnels for ideas, as well as babble and heavy metal. That the mind, like a cluttered slate, can be wiped clean at a stroke and impressed with a message of sweeping consequence, in a language so beautiful it steals the breath.

This is me back in Fantasyland, where crystal balls abound: I see the day when sports fans pour out for poetry events, and vice-versa. I see a gentle awakening, a turning from old modes, a recognition of crying needs: to covet Earth and give children a chance.

As crystals suspended gel before snapping into place, poems abide in (almost) every mind alive. If we all leave poems behind, those who follow will be handed clues to what's important, and what's not. The past will do more to explain itself.

Poetry is being written, and appreciated, by people who may never rise to poetry's pantheon, but are blessed with curiosity . . . a sense of the world around them . . . something to say . . . a need to be heard. These are the audiences great poets dream of — the hope of the future.

David Hedges, president of the Oregon State Poetry Society, has extended its horizons considerably. He organizes both fall and spring poetry conferences and in June of 2002 coordinated the first ever, and highly successful, National Federation of State Poetry Societies Convention held in Coos Bay, Ore. The author of several poetry chap books, David is a contributor to numerous anthologies and journals.

What's Love Got to Do With It

By Stella Cameron and Jennifer McCord

Heroines in our own time. A grand claim, but true of so many who have lived the privilege of discovery, the metamorphosis of the romance genre in the past two decades. Why heroines? Because we have had the courage to embrace stories about the greatest gift, one that cannot be bought or sold, the emotion called . . . love. Together with an estimated 41 million readers in North America whose purchases of romance novels constitute 54.5% of paperback popular fiction and 38.5% of all popular fiction including paperback, hardcover, and trade book ($1.52 billion in annual sales, RWA National 2001 report) sold in this country, Stella Cameron and Jennifer McCord are romance devotees. And, yes, we are heroines of today who, as a writer, and a reader/publishing consultant, celebrate a connection with the heroines and heroes from age to age who are at the heart of every love story.

Stella Cameron, writer:

All fiction genres adhere, even if loosely, to recognizable structures. One constant throughout genre fiction is relationship. Relationships in various guises create basic conflict and heighten the stakes, no matter the vehicle (genre). Successful romance stories hold a relationship between a man and a woman as the core conflict — all other story elements exist to inspire, threaten and fulfill this alliance.

Every writer has a personal story, a tale about one scribbler's journey. My professional journey began in 1980. During the day I made time for two writing sessions, one from 4 to 7 in the morning, one in the late afternoon or early evening. The early morning session never varied unless someone was deathly ill.

Gradually the mountain of manuscript grew, short story on short story, reminiscence on reminiscence, and the mountain occupied cardboard boxes from which I rarely retrieved as much as a single sheet of paper. I knew what I was doing. Pushups. Those hours and pages represented my efforts to build my writing muscles. It never occurred to me that writing for publication was any less of a skill to be studied and honed than any other. There are very few free lunches in publishing, there never have been — I certainly didn't receive any. But I relished the learning process. For me this meant I took night classes, read many books on craft, and wrote, and wrote, and wrote. No day was complete unless new words were written and nothing has changed the way I feel about this discipline.

Originally I intended to write literary short fiction. After all, that was what I read. My goal was to win an *Atlantic Monthly* Prize. Easy enough, right? I never won an *Atlantic Monthly* prize. But I set myself on a path toward the kind of determination that keeps a writer writing throughout the desperate seasons of rejection. A story was always in progress, and I sent them out. And they came back. I schooled myself not to open what I recognized as another returning manuscript until I'd finished writing for the day. Then I opened the envelope and entered the pit for however long it took before I climbed out again.

I started getting what, in world of literary short fiction, are termed "good rejections."

I started getting what, in world of literary short fiction, are termed "good rejections." Apparently oxymorons aren't a problem in some circles. A good rejection may be scrawled, "Try us again," on the back of your cover letter, or perhaps an attractive note card showing wheat waving in the wind and bearing a cheery note announcing, "Not for us at this time."

When a fellow writing student remarked on the relationships that were a common thread throughout every story I wrote, and suggested I should look at the romance currently being published, I wrinkled my nose as only a self-respecting literary snob could. This same brave writer hung in there and brought me a bag of category romances — Harlequin Superromances. "Read them," she said. "They're simple. I know you could knock out a few of 'em in no time." It's tough to read and hold your nose at the same time, but I was determined then as I am now, so I managed a chapter or two. Then I forgot about holding anything but the book. I liked it. I admired a good deal about the author's technique. I wasn't at all sure I could write a romance but I wanted to try.

After some stumbling starts I did write a romance. The whole novel, and a long novel it was. Apart from my classes, I'd been working alone, but someone who read the book thought it would be a great idea for me to enter the Pacific Northwest Writers' Association contest. I dragged my heels and moaned and grasped at the impossibility of writing a synopsis as my final excuse for refusing, but on the last possible day to mail an entry I managed to put together the first synopsis I'd ever written, and off went my first novel

Windspell took second place in the novel category of the contest and I was truly stunned. I had understood that I would be putting the book into the hands of folk who might have given me nose-wrinkling lessons. Of course I thought I didn't have a chance. I was wrong.

Because of the contest outcome I was approached by the agent who was to represent me for a number of years. Also because of the contest placement, there was interest in the novel before my new agent made even one submission. *Windspell* didn't sell then (it did later), but publishers who read the story asked me to make more submissions. *Moontide* sold within a year, and four more novels were purchased on proposals in the following year. I had been studying and practicing the craft of writing — intensely — for four years.

Passion is a powerful word. Some people wouldn't use it on a bet. They may be the wise ones. Others toss passion around with the kind of gusto that suggests they've never examined either its many meanings, or its potential impact. These are the people I don't turn to for understanding. A final group of folks treat passion with reverence. They're a little frightened by it, a little awed by its subtle guises, but they're very sure it exists and they want part of it.

I started in the first group (the avoiders), skipped the second group entirely (the lucky, light-hearted ones), and landed squarely among those of the third persuasion. I'm a reverent, awed passion-seeker. I use passion in whatever garb it presents, wherever it may hang out, and I'm always on the hunt for any secret hiding places I may have missed.

In my early days of becoming serious about writing I gradually came to know that I didn't just want to write professionally — I wanted it passionately. I didn't fiddle around. I told my family, "I'm going to write for a living," and spent every moment I could steal working toward that end. If I'd known how tough it was then, at the instant when I decided to come out of the closet with my announcement . . . I'd have done it anyway. Writing is a passion with me.

Craft was the easy part. What could be more wonderful than to spend hours writing, and reading about writing, to study Janet

Burroway's *Writing Fiction*, and *Understanding Fiction* by Cleanth Brooks and Robert Penn Warren and to feel passionate about what I learned? Talented writer and teacher Ellie Bainter taught me so much during the earliest years. She introduced me to ideas and references I've found invaluable. I met other writers who couldn't get enough of the bones of writing. Louise Hendricksen, Margaret Chittenden, Willo Davis Roberts, Pamela Toth, Janice Johnson, Barthe deClemens, Virginia Myers, Debbie Macomber, the list is too long to be completed here.

When I placed my feet firmly in the romance camp, I was to meet other writers who became my friends and influenced some of the decisions I made. Jayne Ann Krentz encouraged me to write historicals as well as contemporary romance and romantic suspense. Suzanne Simmons has cheered me on every step of the way, and Ann Maxell is my "voice of reason" and a constant inspiration. In very early days Debbie Macomber gave me advice that every new writer

> *Write a whole book before you try to sell one. Then you'll know if you can write a whole book.*

should put into practice: "Write a whole book before you try to sell one. Then you'll know if you can write a whole book."

Like craft, learning about the publishing business is an ever evolving and integral part of the working writer's life. Ignorance is never bliss in any game one plans to play successfully. Wrong steps may cost valuable chances. A manuscript that languishes in an editor's slush pile is a tragedy that doesn't have to happen. Too often such a simple mistake as submitting to the wrong house or editor, or writing a poorly crafted cover letter or a lousy synopsis may handicap a promising piece of work. What does this have to do with the business? If we know who publishes what and who at a publishing house is most likely to be interested in what we have to offer, we eliminate a great swathe of chance. That's part of learning about the business, and the facts changes almost daily. In time we need to understand the selling process between publisher's reps and accounts, print runs, sell-throughs, publishing plans, incentives to accounts, store placements — this is another long list. And the information is available to those willing, and interested enough to do some homework.

For several years — together with some of my close friends in the business — I've spent a lot of time analyzing this huge genre. What makes it work? Why does it sell in such vast quantities? Who are our readers? What are the parallels between romance literature and trends in contemporary society?

Some might say we're wasting serious thinking time on a fluffy topic. Not so. The romance genre works because it speaks to the basic human need for connection, for security, for hope — for passion in relationship, and passion about relationship.

> Ignorance is never bliss in any game one plans to play successfully.

The genre sells great quantities for the same reason with the added proviso that the substantial and faithful audience proves how great is our need for love. As a romance writer who has written something approaching fifty books, I don't feel that I have limitations on what I may choose to write about within the necessary conventions of the genre, but my constants are that good should always overcome evil, and that love is worth fighting for.

Jennifer McCord, reader,
publishing consultant and columnist

I have read romance books now for over twenty years and write a column for Waldenbooks on upcoming books for the reader. My reading history with the genre began in the late 1970s. I had been ill with a flu that the doctor said would keep me in my bed or resting for about a week. He suggested that I go to the library and find some books to read. I was quite surprised when one of the books turned out to be a hardcover that contained three romances. The stories raised my spirits because they were fun to read with a lighthearted and hopeful ending. And as I returned the books to library I asked the librarian if they had any more. Her response was, yes. And the books that I had just read were called "Harlequin romances." What I didn't know was the books were part of fiction called "the romance genre." I can tell you today what the three novels were and who wrote them.

Romance novels of all kinds have continued to be a mainstay in my reading life. I now work in the publishing business and started my career by working in an independent bookstore in the early 1980s. The store specialized in paperback books with special emphasis on commercial fiction, genre fiction and children's books. The romance genre was well represented with new titles and earlier titles.

During that time, American publishers launched very enthusiastically American women writers. I learned the names for sub-genres and how publishers marketed and sold the romance genre. Such names as Debbie Macomber, Nora Roberts, Jayne Ann Krentz, Julie Garwood, LaVyrle Spencer, Sandra Brown and Stella Cameron entered the romance genre and have since become best-selling authors. I then went on to be national spokesperson for Waldenbooks about the romance genre.

For booksellers, readers and writers there are number of sub-genres within the romance genre. They are defined by setting, period, and length of book or elements from other genres. They include but are not limited to: category or series romances have a set word count, mostly contemporary, some historical and are published monthly in mass-market paperback form. The publishers are Silhouette, Harlequin and Zebra/Kensington.

Contemporary romances are described as occurring now and have the feeling of being in today's world. Futuristic romances have mythical settings or include fantasy in the story line. Inspirational romances can be either contemporary or historical but include religious concepts in the plot. Multi-cultural or ethnic romances feature culturally diverse heroes and heroines. Paranormal romances can have various sub-themes of angels, witches, new age and/or gothic themes, vampires, witches, ghosts, time-travel and immortality. Regencies take place in England's regency time period, which lasts nine years from 1811 to 1820. Romantic suspense romances use elements of mystery and intrigue. As the year 2002 approached, historical novels were expanded to include the late 1930s to early 1940s. Settings can be anywhere in the world. All sub-genre factors play a central part of the love story.

The following publishers release romance books every year in the genre: Avon/Harper/Morrow, the Bertlesmann group of Ballantine, Bantam, Dell, Delacorte, Fawcett, Ivy, and Waterbrook, BET, Bargour, Avalon, Warner, the Pearson group of Berkley, Nal, Dutton, Jove,

Onyx, Putnam, Penguin Signet, and Viking, Pocket/Simon and Schuster, Kensington/Pinnacle/Brava/Zebra, St. Martin/Forge, Dorchester, Harlequin/Silhouette/Mira/Steeple Hill, Bethany House, Genesis, Indigo, Tyndale, and Questar/Multomah.

The writer and the reader are always struggling with that constant quest of discovering what love is. What happens between the opening scenario and the promise of happily ever after is "the rest of the story" left to the author's creative imagination. Readers know this is the rhythm of the story. They look forward to the author's interpretation of this ancient story of love.

Currently Stella Cameron (www.stellacameron.com) writes for Mira Books.

Jennifer McCord was for several years a national spokesperson for the romance book business and managed the national romance expert program for Waldenbook stores. She is currently an independent publishing consultant for national and independent publishers. She has worked in book, audio and video programs and products. She is a past board member and president of the Pacific Northwest Writers Association.

Defining Science Fiction

By Jerry and Kathy Oltion

Defining science fiction is like herding cats. There are as many definitions as there are science fiction writers, and each one leads you in a different direction. About the only thing we all agree on is that the stories should probably have something to do with science and they ought to be fiction.

Even that might be too restrictive, since a story really doesn't need much science to be science fiction. The key might be to think of it as "speculative fiction" rather than science fiction. The writer asks, "What if?" and makes a logical extrapolation from there. Scientific discovery may be the most common theme, but this doesn't exclude alternate history, time travel, or sociological change as driving forces.

The key is that the writer must ask, "What if things were different?" or "What if this goes on?" and the story should explore the ramifications of that question. Thus a story about trading stock market futures on the homeless is just as much science fiction as a story about terraforming Mars.

Because the above definition allows so much latitude, science fiction is generally divided into two broad categories: "hard" and "soft." Hard science fiction deals with technological change, while soft science fiction deals more with the human reaction to that change rather than the technology itself. For instance, a hard science fiction story about the invention of the airplane would focus on the Wright brothers, while a soft science fiction story on the same subject might deal with a stewardess strike.

Fantasy often falls under the science fiction umbrella as well. The dividing line between soft science fiction and fantasy is pretty fuzzy, but the most important difference is that fantasy requires only "internal" consistency; it needn't even pretend to be possible in the real world. In a fantasy story about the airplane, people could fly ornithopters or glue feathers to their arms and flap around under their own power.

The one element besides speculation common to all these sub-genres is that the writer must also attempt to illustrate some aspect of the human condition. Even a tale about aliens on Jupiter needs to resonate with the human reader or it's simply not a story.

It may come as a surprise to people who aren't familiar with the genre, but a science fiction story must also be well written. There's plenty of bad science fiction published, just as there's plenty of bad everything else (Theodore Sturgeon once said, "Ninety percent of science fiction is crap, but then ninety percent of everything is crap."), but your odds of selling a story go up dramatically with quality. Also, science fiction readers are much more discerning than most people give them credit for. If you want to build an audience, you'd better present them with your best work.

. . . there's a

huge market for

short fiction.

Note: written science fiction is orders of magnitude better than what you see on television. With a few notable exceptions ("Babylon 5", three or four episodes of "Star Trek" per season), TV science fiction is written by and for people who don't really understand or appreciate the potential of the genre. Those in the know call that stuff "sci-fi," which is a pejorative term that pretty much means "bad science fiction." In this article we're talking about the good stuff, which devotees take the trouble to call "science fiction" or when they must abbreviate it, shorten to simply "sf."

Despite the requirement that it be good, sf is surprisingly easy to sell. There are millions of fans, and dozens of publishers devoted to the genre. Plus, unlike in most other genres, there's a huge market for short fiction. Beginning writers can hone their skills a short story at a time rather than invest a huge amount of effort in a novel while they're still learning. For that reason, short fiction is often considered the best way to break into the field. It's certainly not the only way, but it is easier for most people. Short fiction is the way both of us got started.

Jerry began selling in 1981 to *Analog* magazine and has continued selling short stories there and to other magazines ever since. (He's now got over 80 publications.) He wrote his first novel after his ninth story sale. Kathy sold her first story to a Star Trek contest for new writers. Then, she sold a story to *Analog*. She was still eligible the next year for the Star Trek contest, so she wrote another story for that and sold it, too. She has no immediate plans to write a novel, preferring to gain experience through her short fiction until she feels ready to take on a bigger project.

As Kathy discovered, contests are an especially good market for new writers. (Not contests that charge entrance fees; avoid those like the plague.) There are two major contests for sf: the above mentioned Star Trek: Strange New Worlds and Writers of the Future. Both contests are open only to people who have published fewer than three stories or one novel. Both offer good pay (better than the magazines) and excellent publicity. Plus you're not competing with the likes of Harlan Ellison and Robert Silverberg.

If the above names mean nothing to you, then the first thing you must do before you even begin to write a science fiction story is to read. Read everything you can get your hands on. Read the old stuff (go to a library and look up Andre Norton, Robert Heinlein, and Poul Anderson). Read the new stuff (Tim Powers, Stephen Baxter, Connie Willis, or any current magazine). Read it until you know in your bones what it is and why you want to write it.

. . . once you know instinctively what sf is, you'll never lack for an idea ever again.

That brings us to the dreaded question most often asked of any sf writer: Where do you get your ideas? Any experienced writer dreads the question because the answer is so easy but so hard to make anyone who must ask it understand. You get ideas from reading other stories and wishing the author would have done them differently. You get ideas from hiking in the woods, and from the shapes of clouds on a summer day. You get ideas from the bewilderment (or the comprehension) you feel when you see the inner workings of an automobile engine. You get ideas from your mother-in-law's cooking. Ideas are everywhere, and most sf writers will tell you that the problem is not how to find them but how to make them "stop!"

That may not sound helpful to those of you who are just starting out, but trust us on this: once you know instinctively what sf is, you'll never lack for an idea ever again. Ideas are everywhere. Look: On the desk before us is a computer mouse. What if computer mice were actually alien life forms? There's a business card beside the mouse. What if people in the future needed cards with their names and professions on them so they could remember who they were supposed to be each day? There's a model Volkswagen atop the monitor. What if that was really our car, which we shrink and keep inside when we're not using it? And so on, everywhere you look.

Of course an idea by itself is not enough. As with any other genre, you need good characters in an interesting situation with an equally interesting problem to solve. What sets sf apart is the world in which these characters and their problems exist. The setting possibilities are endless. You can make up pretty much anything you want as long as you can make it believable and relevant to the theme. If you intend to focus on the dark side of genetic manipulation, for instance, you'd be better off setting the story in a 21st century laboratory rather than medieval England. This is not to say that you can't set it in medieval England, but if you do it's going to be more difficult to convince the reader that you know what you're doing.

That's probably the easiest trap to fall into in this business: losing your credibility through carelessness. Science fiction readers are generally well-educated; they will catch you if you make mistakes. They will tell you so, too. It's not so much that they want to embarrass you as it is that mistakes blow their suspension of disbelief and ruin the story for them, so they want to make sure you don't do it again.

Does that mean you have to write what you know? Not at all. That hoary old advice is for the timid! Scientists don't explore what they already know, and science fiction writers shouldn't feel compelled to either. Stretch a little. If your story idea demands that you know about the real-life effects of quantum physics, read Stephen Hawking's books on the subject or find someone who already knows something about it and buy them lunch in exchange for information. A lot of people dread doing research, but that's because they treat it like work. That's silly. Research is the fun part! For one thing, you'll probably find your next dozen story ideas on the way to looking up something else, and for another, the sense of wonder you get when you learn something new will find its way into the story, and your readers will pick up on it.

"Sense of wonder" is hard to define, but it's probably the most important ingredient in any sf story. That's why most people read the stuff. As Greg Benford once said, "Science fiction is for people who want to make their heads feel funny without drugs."

So to recap, here's what you need in order to write science fiction:

- Background knowledge of the sf field.
- An element of speculation (i.e. an "idea").

- Believable characters.
- An interesting (and believable) setting.
- An interesting (and believable) plot.
- Relevance to today's readers.
- Sense of wonder.

Piece of cake, right? It really is. Honest. As with anything that's worth doing, it requires some knowledge and practice, but sf is no harder than any other genre. It's just different. And as we said earlier, one aspect of the job is relatively easy: selling.

Science fiction magazines came into existence in the 1920s with *Amazing*, which is still publishing today. That and three other magazines that came later make up the "old guard," the four that pretty much define the genre. Those four are *Amazing, Analog, Asimov's,* and *The Magazine of Fantasy & Science Fiction*, which everybody just calls *F&SF*. They've been joined by *Aboriginal SF*, *Science Fiction Age, Realms of Fantasy*, Marion Zimmer Bradley's *Fantasy* Magazine (affectionately known as MZB), and a host of others that come and go.

Every one of these magazines is open to new writers.

Every one of these magazines is open to new writers. Better than that: every one of them is *eager* to publish new writers. Why? Because experienced writers tend to move on to novels, leaving the magazines searching for bright newcomers to fill their pages. If they catch a hot one (maybe you!) early on, they'll be assured of at least a couple years of good fiction from you before you too become so swamped with novel deadlines that your story production dwindles.

You don't need an agent. Few good agents (notice the adjective!) will handle short fiction anyway. All you need is a current market listing (which is why you won't find addresses here — they change from time to time) and some sense of what kind of story each magazine is interested in. Some publish only hard sf, some only soft, some only fantasy. Once again, research! Before you mail out anything, read at least one issue of as many different sf magazines as you can so you'll know what you're dealing with.

Once you've picked your market, simply mail the story to the editor. Of course you should put it into proper manuscript format first. This is vital. It's the first thing the editor sees, and it will predispose them to think of you as either a professional or an amateur before they even read a word. (If you don't know what the proper format is, there are countless books on the subject. More research!)

A cover letter is not necessary. Resist the urge to write one unless there is a good reason to. More writers shoot themselves in the foot trying to be witty in a cover letter than with mistakes in the story itself. If you just don't feel complete without one, say, "Dear [Editor's name], Here is my latest story, "[Title]," for your consideration. Thank you." That's really all you need to say, because if the story can't sell itself, it won't sell no matter what your cover letter says. Remember an SASE. Marking your manuscript "Disposable copy" and including just a #10 SASE for the editor's reply is okay if you want to save postage.

The best way to find a good agent is to ask other writers who they recommend.

SF editors don't like simultaneous submissions, so pick your markets carefully and send your story to one at a time. Don't sit around watching the mailbox; improve your chances of selling something by writing more stories and sending them out, too.

All of the above advice applies to novels as well, except for the bit about agents. You don't need an agent to sell a science fiction novel, but it helps. Most book editors take forever to reply to "over the transom" submissions, and because they don't want simultaneous submissions either, it can take years to market your own novel. An agent *can* simultaneously submit, at least in some cases, and they will also know who is most likely to buy your novel in the first place.

The best way to find a good agent is to ask other writers who they recommend. Get ready to hear an earful; writers either love or hate their agents, and in either case they'll talk about them at length if you get them started. Once you've found someone who comes highly recommended, write to them and tell them so, and ask if they're taking on new clients.

How do you find other writers to ask? Easy! There's a science fiction convention going on somewhere nearly every weekend. Everybody goes to them — writers, editors, agents and fans — and everybody is approachable. These aren't stuffy literary conferences with scheduled meetings and lectures; these are big, happy parties where everybody lets their hair down and gets to know one another. If you start attending, you can't help but meet people. Among them will not only be your future agent, but future editors, collaborators, and probably even your spouse.

We aren't kidding. Once you start into this field you will find yourself immersed in it. You will live and breathe it. It will expand your consciousness and alter your perception until the only people who truly share your world view will be other science fiction fans. Everything else will seem . . . well . . . mundane.

Kick back and enjoy the ride. You might as well. Resistance is futile.

A dedicated writer, Jerry Oltion's published novels includes two Star Trek books, Abandon in Place, Twilight's End, Mudd in Your Eye *and* The Getaway Special. *He has over 70 stories published in science fiction magazines and anthologies. Jerry and Kathy, a writer and medical technologist, live in Eugene, Ore.*

True Tales in Screenwriting

By Mike Rich

There is a reason why I try to return every phone call I receive from aspiring screenwriters. It's simple. It's because one year ago I knew the feeling of placing phone call after phone call, and getting nothing after nothing. No calls back, scripts returned still in their original envelope.

And when the aspiring screenwriters call, I tell them what I found out for myself last year: that each success story is different, and that a wonderful script has to be accompanied by a sizable dose of good timing and good luck.

Is my screenplay, "Finding Forrester," that much better than the countless others that remain sealed on their FedEx journey? Of course not. So how did my screenplay sell? Here's the remarkable story of what happened between May and November of 1998.

I wrote "Finding Forrester" during my off-hours at KINK FM radio in Portland. Keep in mind that my on-hours at KINK are 3:15 am to 11 am, Monday through Friday, and my kids get home from school at 2:30 pm. The math's pretty simple. I had a couple of hours on the weekdays and a handful of hours on the weekend. "Forrester" came together in a year.

In short, "Finding Forrester," — another one of those nasty verb "ing"-modifier titles — tells the story of a young black kid from Brooklyn who cultivates a learning relationship with an elderly reclusive author; a man who wrote one of the great novels of his time.

The name of "Forrester," by the way, is a tribute to my high school English teacher, Sharon Forster (yes, we fiddled with the spelling because it looked better,) who inspired me to write during my days at Enterprise High School in eastern Oregon.

I broke every rule. I've never been to Brooklyn and I've never been black. So much for writing what you know.

To make matters even worse, I wrote about a great writer. It was a move I would hesitate to make now, but at the time, it was all merely a story I never dreamed would reach any serious desks.

I was right. The phone was silent, the faxes and letters were one-way trips to agents, studios and producers. And it was right about that time I received a key bit of advice from my friend David Woolsen.

David was the head of the Oregon Film and Video Division at the time. There are a handful of producers and agents that will read unsolicited screenplays but many aren't big enough to generate the proper level of interest.

So David gave me the nugget of advice that got things rolling. If I had enough confidence in my screenplay, try entering it in a *reputable* screenplay contest; and I underline the word "reputable."

I entered three with solid reputations: the Nicholl competition, sponsored by the Academy, the Austin Heart of Film contest and the annual competition at Disney. All have web sites on the Internet.

I waited for the inevitable rejection letter, the one that starts off with something along the lines of "while your story is certainly heartfelt . . . blah, blah, blah . . ." and ends with a most sincere thank you. On July 27th, the letter arrived, but much to my surprise and delight, it was a letter

. . . champagne corks littered the floor of the Rich household for days.

informing me that I had been selected as one of 225 quarter-finalists. Considering that 4500-plus screenplays had been entered, champagne corks littered the floor of the Rich household for days.

On August 18th the next letter arrived; semi-finalist, down to 112 scripts. On September 24th; finalist, 11 scripts. And on October 26th the final letter arrived; fellowship recipient, one of five screenplays selected.

The phones that had been silent were now buzzing with 30 calls a day. Heavyweight agencies, production companies, even studios were inquiring. The champagne corks were becoming a household safety hazard.

A side-note to all of this: I changed my cover letter when I was selected as quarter-finalist and started getting interest at that point. Don't wait until the contest is over. If you get any independent reinforcement of your talent . . . put it in 36 point font at the tip of your letter and use it, use it, and use it some more.

Make your push with the agencies, not with the production companies. One good agent can put your screenplay on dozens of producer's desks; one good production company will make sure it never leaves the office.

I signed with United Talent Agency in November, thinking we'd make a move with "Forrester" in a month or two. I couldn't have been more wrong.

Two days later my script was put up for auction and within 24 hours Columbia Pictures purchased it. Laurance Mark ("As Good As It Gets," "Jerry Maguire") was brought on as producer and Sean Connery agreed to the lead role, while taking on the role of executive producer.

I assumed my work was done, and once again, I assumed wrong.

. . . once again,

I assumed wrong.

All screenwriters dream of selling their script, but what many don't realize (at least I didn't) is that the sale is only the launching pad for re-writing after re-writing after re-writing. One week after the sale of my screenplay I found myself sitting in a conference room at Columbia Pictures across the table from a group of studio executives and producers.

For the next three hours I listened and watched as my script was calmly, almost surgically, picked apart.

"Let's turn to page 46. Is Geoffrey doing this intentionally or by accident?"

"Can we discuss making him a couple of years older? He seems a little young to be doing this."

After three hours they asked me, I'm still not sure how seriously, if I wanted to throw up. I laughed, a physical response that may have kept their question from receiving an all too literal response.

I went in hearing the horror stories of Hollywood studio execs but to be perfectly honest, my experience with Columbia has been a marvelous one. Studio head Amy Pascal and the executives who surround her have developed a reputation as a "writer's studio." It is a reputation I have no trouble believing.

There is, however, an inherent danger in having "too many cooks in the kitchen." What began as a hobby (which I could abandon for two or three weeks at any time) suddenly became a business of deadlines and precise recommendations.

If there is one lesson I've learned over the past year, it's that there is no such thing as a perfect first draft. Someone once told me that when it comes to writing — whether it be novels or screenplays — "don't look back." I assumed it was a rhetorical comment, but it turned out to be a literal one.

"Don't look back" means: Don't stop on page ten of your first draft and start tweaking. If you worry about writing perfect page one, you'll never get to page two.

I'm not discounting the importance of presenting a quality product, just keep in mind that your first draft won't be your last. Studio executives will tell you that when they buy a first draft "spec" screenplay, they're only buying a concept, nothing more.

Unfortunately, there isn't a "Hollywood 101" class. I've always bought into the idea that "ignorance is bliss." But after a while, ignorance is just ignorance. Having never taken a screenwriting class, I didn't realize there is a golden rule on antagonists.

> *Unfortunately, there isn't a "Hollywood 101" class.*

You should have three: an internal antagonist in your main character, an antagonist within the group, and an antagonist outside of the group. The studio still doesn't know (unless they read this piece) that I followed that rule only through blind luck.

Don't concern yourself with writing in a particular genre. If you're sure the industry is buying a specific genre (teen thrillers, young romantic comedies), it'll be buying something else by the time you finish your draft.

Write what you want to write. And please, please, don't narrow yourself to the old saying "write what you know." As I mentioned earlier, I wrote about a black kid from Brooklyn who's a genius, even though I've never been to Brooklyn, never been a genius, and never been black.

Screenplays give you *license*. The things you can imagine, the things you want to imagine — those are the things you can create in 120 pages.

The most satisfying moment will always be the evening you sit down with a glass of wine or a cup of coffee and read your first draft. It's the one moment in which there are no editors (yet), no critics, and no rewrites. It is your story.

Making movies is a messy business, but writing screenplays doesn't have to be. My wife once told me, long before "Forrester" sold, that the worst case scenario is that I'd end up with a story that my children could read years from now. I can think of worse scenarios.

I was fortunate. A studio executive recently told me that what happened with "Forrester" happens about once out of every 40,000 screenplays, that the dream of writing and then selling a script is so seldom realized.

But it happened for me. And if it can happen for a regular guy in Portland, Ore., it can happen again to someone else. Write from the heart and rewrite from the head. Get to page 120. Don't look back.

And when you finally sell your screenplay, celebrate big that first evening. Because even though the dream's been realized the work is just beginning.

Since the completion of the film, "Finding Forrester," directed by Gus Van Sant, which Sean Connery produced and starred in, Mike Rich has written the screenplay for the film, "The Rookie." It is based on the life of comeback baseball pitcher Jim Morris, and produced by John Lee Hancock and starring Dennis Quaid.

Writing Children's Literature: Just Do It

By Susan Blackaby

Defining Children's Literature: Picture This

The wide range of writing that comprises children's literature as a body of work is easier to recognize than it is to define. Consider how far a category has to stretch to accommodate *Sylvester and the Magic Pebble* and *Hatchet*, or *Roll of Thunder, Hear My Cry* and *Lottie's New Beach Towel*, or *The Stinky Cheese Man* and *The Watsons Go to Birmingham — 1963*, or *Blueberries for Sal* and *In the Night Kitchen*. Indeed, all of these titles are shelved together in libraries and bookstores. It is no wonder, then, that there are nearly as many ways to define children's literature as there are people creating it.

Picturebooks are perhaps the most quintessential form of children's literature. They are old-friend familiar in both style and content. Many of the best of them share certain comfortable characteristics. For example:

- Are animals talking? With few exceptions, the ideas and insights of bears, rabbits and cats are unique to children's literature. At their non-threatening, fuzzy best, animals have universal appeal, they demand the use of imagination and suspension of disbelief, and casting them in human situations puts a comical spin on any predicament. A child riding a bicycle to school may be a promising start in establishing character, setting and plot; change the child to a chipmunk, and the reader or listener is required to pay attention and participate in the world of the story.

- Have you read the story more than once? Have you read it more than once today? Re-readability is another earmark of children's literature. If you have a child handy, then you know that best-loved stories can be read again and again, night after night, without losing one smidgen of their charm. If you remember being a child, then you remember climbing into a lap or onto a chair or under a quilt to have your own favorite stories read and reread.

- Is the book both *short* and *sweet*? Picturebooks have few or even very few words and, apart from the occasional "booger" or "butthead," none of them are bad.

By way of illustrating these picturebook characteristics, *Goodnight Moon,* by Margaret Wise Brown, features a rabbit child preparing to leave the familiar world and journey to the dream world. In millions of households, the book has been read thousands of times as part of the evening ritual, wedged between teeth brushing and the last kiss. It is 130 words long.

Succinctly and eloquently put: "[Books for children], what Ursula Nordstrom called 'only the rarest kind of best,' are keenly attuned to the childlike sensibility, fling open wide the windows of the imagination, touch the heart, delight the ear, and enchant the eye."[1] These criteria can be found in every form and format of children's literature from Pooh Corner to Plum Creek.

Writing Children's Literature: Just Do It

If you are going to write, sooner or later — once you put on your lucky cap, sharpen your pencils, get your favorite pad of paper, fill a big mug with something hot, scoot a comfortable chair into the perfect position, find your special pen, turn on the answering machine, put out the dog, label a blank document "Work in Progress" — you need to get words on paper. If you are not a writer, this is bound to sound flip. But you *are* a writer, and you know just what I am talking about.

On a visit to Portland, Newbery Medalist Christopher Paul Curtis was asked what advice he has for someone who wants to write. This was his answer:

Don't take anybody's advice.
Have fun.
Write every day.

Curtis' First Writing Rule: Forget I Said Anything

There are as many ways to approach writing as there are writers, and each one is likely to swear by his or her method: Get up at dawn and write all morning, write from noon to five, write — walk the dog — write; revise every other day, revise as you go, don't revise until you are finished with your first draft; write an outline, write a detailed outline and stick to it, don't write an outline at all; start with the end and work backward, start in the middle and work both ways, start at the beginning and see where you end up.

Sharon Creech suggests taking naps. Now *that* is good advice.

Curtis' Second Writing Rule: Are We Having Fun Yet?

"Writing is easy. All you do is stare at a blank sheet of paper until drops of blood form on your forehead."[2]

I know about this kind of writing. I've experienced this nitty gritty, teeth gashy, blood-sweat-tears version of word crunching. In fact, I am experiencing twinges of it this very minute. But I do not think it accurately portrays the creative process that is used when writing for children.

In writing for children, the task is to embed incredible, amazing and fanciful things in places and situations that are familiar, concrete and true. Ursula LeGuin calls it "putting imaginary toads in a real garden." Eve Bunting calls it "putting real plums in an imaginary cake." At the same time, the content must be emotional, the vocabulary and sentence structure must be elegant and simple, the word count must be spare, and the pacing must be exact.

> *Creating a picture-book is like trying to write* War and Peace *in haiku.*

Writing for children is not easy, even though many people assume that it is probably a cinch. They either have a child, know a child, or used to be a child, and they believe that this connection is all it really takes to write a children's book. Paula Danziger suggests that they sit down and try it the next time they find themselves with fifteen minutes to spare. Peggy Rathmann has a plate with a daunting but accurate inscription: "Creating a picturebook is like trying to write *War and Peace* in haiku."

OK, so it is really, really, really hard. But even so, if you are staring at the blank sheet of paper and waiting for drops of blood to form, you may be in the wrong genre. Writing for children should be a little sillier. I suggest that you stare at the blank sheet of paper until milk comes out of your nose. That is more like it.

Curtis' Third Writing Rule: Day In, Day Out

Everyone who tells you anything about writing will tell you to write every day. However, they are not very specific about *what* to write, and I long assumed it had to be both substantial and promising, like a *chapter* of something. Then it dawned on me: I write every day for a *living*.

HELLO. I have since come to believe that writing is writing, and short of the grocery list, everything counts. Throw in some well-placed adjectives, a profile of the check-out clerk, a descriptive paragraph about what your refrigerator looks like, and a run through the store from the shopping cart's point of view, and even the grocery list will count.

I usually have a story or two tumbling around, but it can take weeks or even months before I am ready to transform the characters, ideas and episodes into words. By then, I know what is in the character's front hall closet, how she takes her tea, things about her neighbors that drive her crazy, ten projects she is meaning to tackle around her house, and her favorite color.

In the meantime, my work keeps me limber, wordwise. Among other things, I write leveled readers, phonics readers and vocabulary builders for basal reading programs. For these assignments, I am typically given a genre (adventure, mystery, humor), a theme ("children in a family business," "getting to know a grandparent"), a grade level, and a list of five or six vocabulary words (usually unrelated in any meaningful way) that need to be incorporated into a story that averages about 800 words. In the last year, I have written about 25 of these books, and I know that my writing has steadily improved title by title. If you are stuck for something to write about but you know that you need to oil your gears, pick six interesting words and a situation and have at it.

Brainstorming is good, too, even if you think your brain is empty. For one thing, it is a way to fill up a blank page, which is encouraging right there. If you haven't tried it, you will be amazed by how quickly characters and settings can emerge from lists that are totally random and utterly vague: Name, Physical Characteristics, Place, Weather, Mood, Situation, and so on. List several possibilities for each category and then mix and match:

Name	Physical Characteristics	Place
Lori	rosy cheeks	living room
Wendell	blue eyes	school yard
Louise	stringy hair	cafeteria
Ann	freckles	veranda

Weather	Mood	Situation
stormy	cheery	first day of school

hot	blue	moving away
sultry	mad	birthday party
raining	miserable	broken arm

Ann Louise pushed her wet bangs out of her eyes as she waited on the veranda for someone to answer the bell at the Patterson-Glen residence. She could feel her soggy socks soaking into the lining of her party shoes, and the wrapping paper on Cynthia's present was making a little blue puddle on her skirt.

So You Want to Get Published? Join the Club

The first organization you should join if you are interested in writing for children is the Society of Children's Book Writers and Illustrators (SCBWI). It provides a wealth of information and support at all stages of the publishing process, from blank page to bound book. Regional affiliates sponsor workshops, host gatherings and organize critique groups. Annual conferences, both regional and national, give you many opportunities to meet authors, agents and editors and to get your work critiqued. Editors who do not accept unsolicited manuscripts often accept submissions from SCBWI members or from conference attendees. (Membership information can be found at their website, listed below.)

Thanks to a critique by Ann Rider at the 1999 Oregon SCBWI Conference, Houghton Mifflin accepted my picturebook manuscript for publication, so I can personally attest to the dazzling advantages of SCBWI membership.

There are many other organizations in the Pacific Northwest that offer information, inspiration and support to writers in all genres, and these groups also sponsor workshops, conferences, contests and awards and literary grants. They include the Oregon Writers Colony, the Pacific Northwest Writers Association, Willamette Writers and Literary Arts, Inc.

The Haystack Summer Program in the Arts and Sciences at Cannon Beach offers a children's book festival. Special sessions are devoted to writing for children, including an insider's view of the editor's job and the publishing process, invaluable advice and guidance, manuscript or portfolio evaluations, and a marketing overview.

Moving and Shaking

If your name is a household word and your book is on every night-stand in the country, then you can probably spend most of your time gardening, answering mail and working on your next blockbuster. If not, then you'd better put away the trowel and get busy.

Once your book is in the pipeline, start some chatter. Line up contacts. Get the Rolodex spinning. Put the 'net' in network. The distance between writing a book and selling a book is a quantum leap. You will want to get a running start.

> ... *do not assume that your publisher will make anything happen without you.*

In today's marketplace, it is safe to anticipate that your publisher will leave a lot of the legwork up to you, especially if you are, for the time being anyway, an unknown quantity.

When you consider how competitive it is to get your manuscript (a) read, (b) considered, (c) accepted, it is not surprising that the situation does not get any easier when the book is finally published. Most writers are hoping to be authors, and most authors want to be successful, so it is surprising that their attitude toward marketing often ranges from reluctant to unwilling.

Attending author events at conferences, libraries and bookstores will give you ideas on how to create a presentation that will be successful and surefire for your target audience. Appearances can be set up on your own terms according to a timetable that fits your work schedule and accommodates your other obligations. If you feel you are better at writing in your own little world than you are at speaking in the big real world, maybe you need to figure out an interactive comfort zone: Would you rather participate in a panel discussion for 300 or read to a group of ten? Decide on what you can handle and how you want to handle it, find positive strategies for promoting your work, plan to follow through, and do not assume that your publisher will make anything happen without you.

Did I mention setting up a web site? You may write on a yellow legal tablet with a Number Two Ticonderoga, but you are going to have to get linked.

Speaking of Web Sites

The following web sites provide resources that are both helpful and informative. You can also browse the Internet for author sites, which can be found through publishers, through the Children's Literature links, through the Children's Book Council links, and by searching individual names. This list is, of course, by no means exhaustive, but it will get you into the thick of it when it comes to locating writers' resources. Important submission guidelines, contacts and insights, in addition to website URLs and e-mail addresses, can be found in the *Children's Writer's and Illustrator's Market*, which is published annually by Writer's Digest.

American Booksellers Association	www.ambook.org
Association of Booksellers for Children	www.abfc.com
American Library Association	www.ala.org
Children's Book Council	www.cbcbooks.org
Children's Literature	www.childrenslit.com
Haystack Summer Program	www.haystack.pdx.edu
The Horn Book	www.hbook.com
International Reading Association	www.reading.org
Oregon Literary Fellowships	www.literary-arts.org
Oregon Writers Colony	www.oregonwriterscolony.org
Pacific Northwest Booksellers Association	www.pnba.org (under construction)
Publishers Weekly	www.publishersweekly.com
Society of Children's Book Writers and Illustrators	www.scbwi.org
SCBWI — Oregon	www.rio.com/~robink/scbwi.html
Willamette Writers	www.willamettewriters.com

Read On

When you aren't writing, read. Read, read, read. Stay in touch with what is available, what is getting attention and what is selling by visiting the children's section of your local bookseller and keeping up with reviews. Check out what is and is not available at the library. Knowing the corner of the children's market you hope to capture will help you determine how your work fits in and what makes it special.

Ask Yourself...

Are you working on a book about twins in a midland mining town, mice in a medieval castle, time travelers locked onto a space station, or junior detectives at a dilapidated apartment complex with a sinister super? Is your protagonist 10 years old? Will your manuscript be perfect once you cut 500 words out of a 1500-word story? Was your all-time favorite book read aloud to you by your babysitter? Are your literary heroes rodents? Does the thought of a bear in an overcoat throw your imagination into overdrive? Do characters who can fly sound perfectly plausible to you? Well, guess what? You are a children's writer! What could be cooler?

[1] Heather Vogel Frederick, children's writer and book reviewer for *Publishers Weekly*
[2] Gene Fowler

Susan Blackaby has been editing and writing educational materials for nearly twenty years. Her first "real" book, Rembrandt's Hat, *was published by Houghton Mifflin (Spring 2002). She lives and works in Portland with her husband, humor writer and columnist Jeff Shaffer, and their daughter, Rudy.*

The eWriter: Point, Click, Publish

By Jenny Lynn Zappala

Dot Com companies. Web sites. eBooks. The buzz about "New Media" markets, particularly the Internet, is growing as fast as the markets themselves. Soon, the Internet will be a world-wide, mainstream media and it's just the beginning. Walking through an electronic store is like walking through a sci-fi movie: eBooks (www.ebookconnections.com), portable reading devices (www.rocketbook.com), computer games and palm-sized computers.

Telecommunication devices exchange information — content — such as news reports, business articles, home & garden features, and novels. As the demand for content grows, so does the demand for writers. Electronic writers. It might as well be you.

All this technology can sound complicated, but it can also be an adventure and an opportunity. This is an introduction to the market's unique characteristics and challenges as well as a sampling of resources available to aspiring and practicing eWriters. Many of these ideas are Internet related, but also relate to other electronic markets.

What You Already Know Can Help

The good news: If you're already a successful or aspiring print writer, you have the basic skills to be an eWriter. If you have an expertise (parenting, medicine, cooking), you may even be in demand.

"I don't see eWriters as being all that different from traditional writers," said Adam Engst, publisher of the TidBITS Web site and eWriter in his own right. "There are some different rules and the audience can be somewhat different online, but that's not significantly different than the switch from newspaper writing to magazine writing. . . . Quite simply, writing is about communication, and communication is moving online."

Writing still needs to be clear, crisp, clean and concise. The query letter still needs to grab the editor.

"At its core, writing for new media isn't much different from writing for "old-fashioned" media such as newspapers," said Brian Chin, senior producer at Seattle *Post-Intelligencer* online. "Many of the old principles still apply. It's still working with words but sometimes in different ways."

You don't need the latest computer, software or hardware to be effective, but don't let your gear lag much further behind than one or two years. If you're comfortable sending and receiving e-mail and attached files, using a CD-ROM, using a search engine and can find information on the Internet quickly without too much frustration, you are well on your way.

More editors and agents are accepting submissions and queries by e-mail, whether the intended publication is online or print. Be sure to follow guidelines about how to package and send the material. Feel free to ask an editor or agent what information they want in correspondence or submissions.

Above all, if your eWriting sells, it's working. If it doesn't, keep trying.

Walk the Walk

The old rule of "read what you write" is doubly true in this fast-paced market. To capture Web surfers, be one. Take note of what you like and what keeps your attention.

The invention of the ink press led to the creation of new writing forms like the novel and the newspaper. New software and hardware debut everyday and futurists are predicting new writing forms will emerge.

"Current multimedia writing gigs tend to consist of articles — much like print articles, but less linear and more fragmented — or scripts that synchronize or sequence visuals with narration or text," said Lev Liberman, an Internet consultant and new media instructor who teaches at the University of Oregon. "But be aware that these forms — articles and scripts — are holdovers from last century's linear nonfiction media models. . . . The eWriting of the future will be flexible, contextual, experiential, responsive."

"Today's readers and viewers will become tomorrow's correspondents and participants, interacting at will with everybody and everything in their environment: friends and workmates, experts and avatars, even the toaster and the fridge."

Communication predictions are rampant at present. One theory, known as "convergence" or "converging technologies" predicts the communication and media devices such as wireless telephone, cable television, computers and print media will converge into a single portable

THE EWRITER: POINT, CLICK, PUBLISH

device. Serious eWriters should also pay close attention to information architecture, the science of organizing content into logical systems. Both of these theories are widely discussed in popular literature.

Liberman recommended two examples of emerging communication theories: "The Diamond Age," science fiction novel by Neal Stephenson and ananova.com, a Web site with a digital news anchor-woman, an avatar (virtual character) who reads the news.

Talk the Talk

What about all the techno-babble? Feeling techno-phobia? Consider this. For decades, writers have been perfectly capable of print writing without knowing how to hang a plate on a press. In the same way, it is possible to write for electronic media and never learn computer language or know what's under the hood of your computer.

But it doesn't hurt to have an inkling. New media has the capacity to meld words, audio, video and interactive software into a multimedia experience. There is a trend towards interactive multimedia projects that writers, programmers, graphic artists and other talented people collaborate on. It helps writers to be familiar with the range of tools available, including forums, databases and — yes — code.

"Get an idea of the strengths and weaknesses of different tools," said Chin. "You don't need to become an expert in all things, but it will be very helpful if you understand what all the tools can do; it'll help you figure out how to use them and how they can work in tandem with writing."

The Need for Speed

If you think television audiences have a short attention, try Web surfing. Electronic publishing is instantaneous and constant. Some new agencies update their Web sites twice a day or hourly. The fast-paced market means a greater demand for copy and demanding deadlines.

"Learn to write final draft text quickly," said Engst. "Without the artificially imposed deadlines set by the need to print and distribute paper, writing in the new media requires speed and accuracy. And if you can hit all your deadlines with quality text, you'll be extremely popular with editors."

Text should also be tight and bright. Usability studies show new media writing is geared for scanning rather than reading, said Chin.

"The emphasis is on 'quick-hit' presentation. Information needs to be presented quickly and concisely — as a bulleted list on a Web page, or an eight-word headline flashed to a pager," said Chin. "A key tenet of writing new media is conveying the maximum information in the minimum word count," he said.

Using a series of stand-alone paragraphs with sub-headings is a common style. Abbreviated writing styles such as bullet lists, digests, captions, information graphics, charts and tables are also used to present primary information.

Another key difference: interactivity. Readers read print media from beginning to end for as long as their interest holds. On the Net, users point and click their own path through headlines, summaries, related articles and list items. There is no guarantee what path a reader will take.

"People may read it backwards or in pieces," said Liberman. "You can't refer to what you said or what you're about to say. The only thing you know they are reading is what is in front of them."

Organization and navigation become increasing critical.

"'Electronic writers need to take that into account," said Chin. "Often, their job isn't so much to tell stories as to organize information in a way that helps readers evaluate what options are available so they can make better choices about the content they want to see."

Show Me the Money

It's no secret. Publishers are shoveling money into new media projects, on and off the Web, with little direct monetary returns. The projects, however, compliment and promote existing businesses. More companies are willing to pay professional writers for quality writing.

Because Web sites are cheaper and easier for the average Netizen to produce print magazines, eZines (small circulation newsletters) are an explosive growth market. If you want to be published all over the Net, eZines make it possible. To get the paycheck, you have to be picky. Is this an established press? Or a fly-by night operation?

Market listings and submission guidelines, for on- and off-line markets, are available online. If the work is small (a one-shot article for $30) an e-mail or letter describing the scope of work, deadline and payment can be sufficient. For a commission worth $200 or more, a contract will not only protect your interest, but it's also an opportunity to outline expectations for the final product.

"For online content writing jobs, I often invoice based on an hourly fee," said Liberman. "For bigger projects I'll charge a flat fee, offering a substantial discount for half up front. Advance payment is advisable, especially if you're investing a lot of time on research, turning down other work, etceteras.

"Refusal to pay anything up front is often the sign of a shaky Internet startup with scanty cash reserves," added Liberman. "The last time I agreed to do a big slug of work with no advance payment, the company went out of business and left me whistling for my fee. Be afraid. Be very afraid."

Personal Web sites are an effective promotion and marketing tool to advertise tour dates, release sneak peak excerpts and display your portfolio. It's also great practice, said Engst.

"Part of the reason I find writing as easy as I do is that I've written literally thousands of articles for TidBITS over the years," said Engst. "I'd encourage anyone who's breaking into the new media to self-publish articles on a personal Web site, both as a way of generating portfolio material and as a way to get in the groove of writing online."

Many community colleges, libraries and computer users group offer introduction courses about creating and maintaining a personal Web site.

Evading Calamity and Cyber Pirates

The writer's worse nightmare: creating an awesome, cosmic idea that's more poetic, marketable and popular that the Beatles or Star Wars combined — and losing control of the copyright. It's a perception that keeps many writers away from this market; The Internet is a malleable meat market for plagiarists and copycats to cut, paste and steal paragraphs, articles and entire chapters between sips of coffee.

You can protect your reputation, income and hard work by re-acquainting yourself with our dear friend: Mr. Copyright. Writers should understand electronic copyrights before pitching work into the virtual marketplace. The U.S. Copyright Office is online and always open for a quick peek. (www.loc.gov/copyright/) Yea, it's boring and intimidating, but it's important. You have to learn the game to make sure you win, said Kohel Haver, an attorney specializing in intellectual properties.

Point, Click, Begin

eZines and Communities

E-Book Connections:
Browse eBook authors, publishers and links as well as sample reviews and surveys of eBooks. (www.ebookconnections. com)

Inscriptions Magazine:
Weekly eZine for working writers with paying markets, job listings, contests, interviews, articles and industry news. (www.inscriptionsmagazine. com)

Organizations

Author's Guild: A society of published authors, whose Web site offers articles about industry news, electronic rights court decisions and contract advice. Members offered insurance and other benefits. (www.authorsguild.org)

National Writers Union:
A trade union for freelance writers in all genres that offers information, networking, job listings, insurance and benefits to members and non-members. (www.nwu.org)

Search Engines

About.Com: A search engine keeps its lists short and sweet and organized by topics. Forums, chats and job boards also available. (www.about.com)

Code is print. Once a piece is saved to disc, it's the same as if it was written on paper, said Haver. Adding the copyright mark marks your turf and declares an intent to protect the work. For the professional, it's not enough.

Any substantial work should be registered with the U.S. Copyright Office. If you write short articles for a living, Haver recommends registering them in batches roughly once a quarter. If anything happens to a registered piece, you can access the court, recover your lawyer's fees and request compensation above and beyond the value of the work, said Haver. That's well worth the $30 registration fee.

Take extra care in reading contracts before you sign. Publishing runs for print work is limited to editions. Electronic publishing can print infinite copies on Web sites, isolated networks, electronic archives and CD-ROMs. Be sure to ask the company what they intend to do with your piece and for how long, said Haver.

"(The company) should pay (the writer) whenever they use it in a different way and they should let you know when they've made a contract (with someone else.)" said Haver. "You don't ever want to license the rights away . . . and then lose control of it and not be able to track it anywhere else."

Also be cautious if a company offers to market your writing into other mediums, such as a computer game or CD-ROM. Considering limiting the time a company has to market the piece, said Haver.

"It's comforting that someone is going to do that for you, but make sure they are going to do it," said Haver. It's common for companies to "want to own it, but then they sit on it."

Electronic rights are still new and will not settle down for a decade or more. It pays to pay extra close attention. Writers associations, such as the National Writers Union and The Author's Guild, post updates about the decisive court cases happening now.

Writers can also invest in "physical" insurance. Computers are fragile. Heat, cold, water, fire, magnets, unintentional file command — just about anything is a hazard. I can not stress enough the importance of backing up your writing on magnetic tapes, CD-ROMs or other long term data storage regularly. It's also worth printing final drafts and storing them in binders. The notebooks and back up tapes can be kept in a fire-proof box in a bank safe, heated storage or friend or relatives' home.

Learning to Learn

The Net allows writers worldwide to swap ideas and information through writing groups, associations, bulletin boards and chat rooms. Somewhere out there is a forum that's ideal for you and your writing, but it may take some exploration. Use a search engine or ask your colleagues for recommendations.

In a new, fast-paced market it's up to the eWriter to keep pace and take a few creative risks. For many, that's the appeal of electronic markets.

"Top priority for writers: study new media, retool your skill set, find an appropriate area of specialization — or several," said

Ask Jeeves: A search engine questions (such as 'What is a comma used for?') rather than a search string (grammar AND comma). A good engine for generic questions. (www.ask.com)

Dogpile: A meta-search engine that searches more than a dozen common engines at once. If you are looking for something specific, a person or want to get the big picture about "what's out there", try here. (www.dogpile.com)

FindLaw: An example the kind of special interest search engines the Net has to offer. They take time to find, but once found can shave hours off your research time.

WhoIs: This engine answers the age-old question: who really owns this Web site. This search will show you who registered the Web site, their address, contact information and other neat info. (www.networksolutions.com /cgi-bin/whois/whois)

Books

Kirsch's Handbook of Publishing Law: For Author's, Publishers, Editors and Agents Acrobat Books, 1994 ISBN: 0918226333

How the Internet Works Preston Gralla Macmillan Computer Publishing, 1996 ISBN: 1-56276-404-7

Interactive Writer's Handbook
Darryl Wimberley and
  John Samsel
Carronade Group, 1996
ISBN: 1-885452-11-X

*Labyrinths: The Art
of Interactive Writing
and Design*
Domenic Stansberry
Integrated Media
  Group, 1998
ISBN: 0-534-51948-2

Writing for Multimedia
Timothy Garrand
Focal Press, 1997
ISBN: 0-240-80247-0

Liberman. "Re-engineer yourself; the gigs will follow."

Sources

Brian Chin is senior producer at the Seattle Post-Intelligencer's *new media department and a 1997 New Media Fellow from the Newspapers Association of America. (www.seattle-pi.com)*

Adam C. Engst, publisher of the Internet newsletter TidBITS for over ten years, has written numerous magazine articles and books, including the best-selling Internet Starter Kit series. (www.tidbits.com/adam)

Kohel Haver, an attorney who specializes in intellectual properties and copyright law, is on the Computer & Internet executive committee for the Bar Association of Oregon.

Lev Liberman, an interactive creative director and Web consultant, teaches new media writing and information architecture courses at University of Oregon, and has created award-winning corporate and entertainment Web sites. (levulus@home.com)

About the Author

Jenny Lynn Zappala has worked as a reporter at The Daily World *in Aberdeen, Wash., and is a freelance writer. She earned an interdisciplinary degree from Western Washington University, titled "Journalism, Publishing and Web Content Development."*

Mark Russell's Top 10 Zines of the Northwest!
(In no particular rank or order)
By Mark Russell

Defined: A Zine is any collection of literary or graphic art published without the assistance of a professional publisher. It is usually self-published by the author of the material or someone equally hapless in the art of commercial publication.

1. Dishwasher

Our hero, known only as Dishwasher Pete, chronicles his ambition to wash dishes in all fifty states. His adventure takes him across America to diners, restaurants, an oilrig and it eventually earns him an appearance on the David Letterman Show, where one of his friends goes on the air in his place and demonstrates to Letterman the act of lighting his own hand on fire.

2. Journal of Ride Theory

Published by Dan Howland of Portland, Ore., this fanzine is dedicated to amusement park rides. Howland features commentary on rides of the past, present and a few ill-advised, futuristic rides that were never built, such as a Ferris wheel, which rolls up and down a rollercoaster track. Known to include the occasional diatribe against Disney theme parks.

3. The Patricia Letters

Published by Spokane, Wash., native Kevin Sampsell, The Patricia Letters (PUT IN ITALICS) is a funny, yet very moving portrait, told in an epistolary format, of a poor rural ex-con trying to win the approval of his soon-to-be stepdaughter.

4. Eyeheart Everything

This collection of short stories, vignettes and esoterica by Mykle Hansen includes the story of cratchaflatch, a little-known and rarely-used obscenity who is embittered by the neglect he is shown by an indifferent public and consumed by his envy of the dirtier, more popular obscenities of modern vernacular.

5. Please Don't Kill the Freshmen

A fifteen year-old girl, writing under the alias of Zoe Trope, recalls her freshman year of high school in a languid, poetic stream-of-consciousness style of writing that will leave you dumbfounded. It is soon to become a novel.

6. Peterson's Incident Report

Compiled by Ms. George Black, this zine is a collection of anecdotes written by the employees of an all-night convenience store detailing the funny and mysterious antics of the would-be shoplifters, drunks and crazies that come in after hours. All proceeds from the zine go to Portland, Ore., area homeless shelters.

7. Farm Pulp

Published by Greg Hischak out of Seattle, Wash., this is a humor-oriented zine primarily populated by amusing short stories and essays peppered with clip-art. It may come in a yellow cover, because Greg once got a really great deal on yellow paper.

8. Girl Juice

Published by Heavy Flow, a sub-division of Future Tense Press dedicated to women writers, Girl Juice is a collection of short stories written by Ritah Parrish. Each story contains wickedly sharp wit, richly developed characters and at least one reference to a wholly unnatural sex act.

9. Jar of Pennies

Published By Kalah Allen. It is a collection of little vignettes of everyday life, told in comic book form. Her warm and rounded style of drawing underscores the feeling of depth and humanity that permeates these brief snapshots of human existence.

10. The Penny Dreadful

I've got a lot of damn nerve, putting my own zine on a list of my favorite zines. A lot of damn nerve. But aside from the fact that I am an egomaniac, I wanted everyone to know about The Penny Dreadful, issue #17, because it includes several excellent contributions from the aforementioned Kevin Sampsell and Mykle Hansen, and the previously unmentioned Eugene-native Bryce Ingman.

Most of the zines contained within this list are available in Seattle at Elliott Bay Books, in Portland at Reading Frenzy or Powell's. They can also be ordered on-line at www.powells.com.

Editor's note: We encourage Seventh Edition readers to go out to this wonderful website. However, don't get lost and forget to return. The possibilities for good information for writers are endless on this website.

Mark Russell is a writer and cartoonist living in Portland, Ore. Currently, he publishes his work in his zine The Penny Dreadful *and on his website www.hevanet.com/pendread.*

"Writing is one of the few professions left

where you take all the responsibility for what you do.

It's really dangerous and

ultimately destroys you as a writer

if you start thinking about responses to your work

or what your audience needs."

Erica Jong

Writing Resources

Revision Tips

Author, teacher M.K. Wren has conducted hundreds of workshops and classes for writers. She shares the following two lists that have proven most helpful to writers.

Vagueness: Not: She looked strange. Be specific. Her greenish skin emphasized her glazed, red-rimmed eyes.

Unintentional repetition: He left me there nursing a broken left arm.

Unnecessary or trite adjectives and adverbs: The blue sky was very beautiful.

People are *who*, not *that:* The woman who stole the cream smiled.

UFAs: Unidentified flying Antecedents: Tom, Dick, and Harry went to *his* house. Too many participial phases. Opening the door, Tom walked into the house and stopped abruptly when he saw the body. Hurrying to catch up with Tom, Dick almost ran into him. Recognizing the blood corpse, Harry fainted.

Dangling participles: Lying on the parquet floor, Tom stared at the body.

Lack of variety in form: All your paragraphs are five lines long; all your sentences are declarative — or worse, begin with participial phrases.

Digressions: Exquisite prose that has nothing to do with the story.

Expository lumps: Beasties that go bump in the narrative.

Stilted dialogue: Use contractions and listen to the way people talk.

Sluggish pacing: Usually due to too much detail in the wrong place.

Lack of chronological and logical order: Jane screamed. She turned on the light and saw Tom, Dick, and Harry huddled over the body.

Portent of doom: Little did she know….

Hopefully: You can pray hopefully, but the rain won't stop hopefully.

As in the sense of *because* or *since*: Yes, as it's in the dictionary, it's correct, but it has an old-fashioned and pedantic sound.

Done: A task can be done, but not a person — unless he or she is being prepared as a feast for cannibals.

Which and *that* are not interchangeable. (Check restrictive and nonrestrictive clauses.) Neither are the verbs *lay* and *lie*, or *sit* and *set*.

In dialogue, lagging attributives: Get them in early before reader decides someone else is saying these words.

Serial comma: His diet consisted of nuts, raw fish, and peanut butter sandwiches.

Scenes in limbo: Always provide the reader a particular place and time to be in.

Avoid exclamation marks! Except judiciously in dialogue.

Do's and Don'ts for Writers

1. Don't pursue writing because you expect to produce a best-seller and become a millionaire. Buy a lottery ticket. The odds are better.

2. Do learn your craft, and that includes such nitty-gritties as punctuation. Commas are as important to meaning as words.

3. Don't forget that the first draft is just the beginning, and you'll seldom write so much as a sentence that can't be improved.

4. Don't attempt to write a particular kind of story because you think it will sell. It probably won't.

5. Do write the kind of stories you love to read. A novel is a consuming, sometimes harrowing undertaking that will likely take years to complete, so you'd better enjoy what you're writing about.

6. Do embrace your characters and their problems and their world passionately. If you don't care about them, how can you expect anyone else to care?

7. Don't be afraid to submit your story to editors and agents. The worst they can do is to say no. As devastating as that may be, you've at least had the learning experience of writing a completed novel. Besides, there are other editors and other agents. And if they all reject your manuscript, there are other stories for you to write.

8. Do keep a few ideas simmering on the back burners of your mind, and as soon as you finish one story, begin the next. The wheels of publishing grind exceedingly slow, if not exceedingly fine. You can't wait to find out if your first manuscript will be accepted before you start the next one.

9. Do consider preparing for writing your novel with a working notebook: that is, studies of your main characters, maps and floor plans of sites where most of the action takes place, a scene-by-scene synopsis, etc. It might save you a couple of drafts.

10. Do remember that it's possible that you're not cut out to be a writer. This is not evidence of your failure as a human being. If your talents lie elsewhere, you've lost nothing by learning about the craft of writing. In fact, you may have gained a great deal.

Northwest Freelance Rate Chart

Advertising copywriting $300-$800 (fractional page to full page)

Annual Reports $1500-$5000

Articles $450 (up to 1000 words), $500-$800 (up to 1500 words), $800-1500 (2000-3000 words)

Books — Ghosted — Negotiated contract

Brochures $400-$800 for tri-fold; $125-$250 per page for full size page

Business letters — Charge hourly rates

Company newsletters, desktop publishing plus some writing, $250-$500 per page; $20-$80 per hour for writing, editing

Corporate history — Negotiated contract

Editing (copy) $50-$80 per hour; as low as $12 away from the urban centers

Editing (major) $50-100 per hour

Family History — Negotiated contract

News releases $30-$50 (1-2 pages)

Promotional or public relations $50-$100 per hour

Research for writing projects $20 per hour

Resume writing $25-$50

Website management $50-$75 per hour

Writing/publishing consulting $75-$125 per hour

Note: Depending upon individual billing practices these prices may or may not include out-of-pocket expenses such as mileage, travel expenses, long distance calls, time spent on e-mails, faxes,

This list was compliled by Myrna Daly, Carmel Bently, Sally Petersen and several responders from Oregon Press Women.

Query Letter How-To

By Marlene Howard,
Media Weavers/Writers Northwest Publisher

A query letter is a writers' sales letter. You write a query letter to get the attention of an agent or to sell an article or story idea to an editor. Every writer needs to learn how to write a good query letter.

The following are the basic must-do rules for query letters:

- The query letter must be perfect. This means no typos, spelling or grammar errors.

- The query letter must be only one page. This is good practice for editing your own work. Learn to say what you have to say in concise language.

- The query letter is a business letter. Use standard business letter form. It is not a friendly, chatty letter. Address the letter to a specific person. Take the time and do the research to find out who is the best person to receive your query.

- Business letters do not have to be boring. This is where you show your writing skill. Think about it, wouldn't an editor or agent doubt a writer's ability to make 50 to 400 pages interesting if he or she can't even hold their interest for one page.

- Send a self-address stamped envelope (SASE).

- Try to avoid all clichés.

What should you include in a query letter?

- You have to tell what the book or article is about. This may mean reducing an intricate 300 page book to a maximum of two paragraphs. This is where you show your skill to choose only the "telling" details.

- You have to tell why you are the person to write this book. Show your credentials or your passion, but convince your reader that only you can write this book.

- You have to tell why readers will want to read this article or buy this book. Don't tell them that your market is everyone. Not so. Show that you understand and are aware of different genres, interest groups, or politics. How do they affect the market for your book?

As in any piece of writing the first paragraph must hook your reader. This paragraph could be:

- Narrative — must have punch, drama, or shock power.
- Anecdote — a short story.
- Quote — Good if the person quoted is well known.
- Premise — what the story is really about.

Practice writing a query letter for each piece of writing you complete. The query letter may be the single most important piece of writing you ever do. Take time to think about what can go into your letter that will not only talk about your writing project, but will show your writing skill.

We suggest you try to collect good query letters that have worked. You can find these in books and writers' magazines. Or if you have an opportunity to talk with published authors at a class or conference you might ask them if they would share one of their successful query letters. Build up a collection and study why they work. Compare your own rejection letters to successful ones and determine how you can improve them.

This seems a good place to offer one of our favorite quotes from Elements of Style, William Strunk, Jr.

"Omit needless words. Vigorous writing is concise. A sentence should contain no unnecessary words, a paragraph no unnecessary sentence, for the same reason that a drawing should have no unnecessary lines and a machine no unnecessary parts. This requires not that the writer make all his sentences short, or that he avoid all detail and treat his subjects only in outline, but that every word tells."

Self-Publishing

By Marlene Howard,
Media Weavers/Writers Northwest Publisher

The editors of this book would not presume to tell you how to self-publish. There are many excellent books already available that can actually help you through the entire process. However, we offer the following basic guidelines you can use to research before you make the final decision to self-publish.

Self-Published Authors

Talk to at least eight authors who have published their own work. This should be in person, not on the internet. Keep in mind that once authors have published their books they are in a marketing mode and by definition that mode must be positive. Therefore their websites and e-mails are meant to encourage readers to buy their books.

Some of the better places to meet self-published authors are writers groups, conferences, and formal organizations for self-publishers. (You can find some of these listed in this book on page 124). Questions to ask are:

Why did you decide to self-publish?

Some negative reasons to watch for might be:
> "book had been rejected by dozens of agents and editors and I just wanted to do it."

Positive reasons could be:
> "When I gave a presentation at a conference many audience members asked me where they could buy copies of my material."

Take careful notes and see if your own reasons match any of theirs.

How long did it take to complete the process?

You may want to buy the books or get them from libraries and judge for yourself if this author's work could have benefited from an editor before you ask this question.

Did they use a freelance editor?

Ask the following questions only if you like the appearance of the book.

Who did their book design work?
Where did they get the book printed?
How many did they have printed?

And the final question is:

How is it selling?

This question you may have to answer yourself. If you can find the book in book stores and libraries, then it is probably doing OK. Or if the author talks about reprints or when the next book will come out.

Book Stores

Talk to at least 4 independent book store owners about how they buy self-published books. Ask them about POD (Print on demand.) Independent book stores are important for self-publishers and you must find out how best to sell them your book before you begin your project.

If you have a favorite chain bookstore you might also ask to speak to a store supervisor or manager and find out how they would acquire a local author's self-published book.

Web-based stores and websites

Again, ask other authors who you know and trust. Do they actually sell enough books on the internet to support the publication?

Make sure that after you publish the book you will be able to find a place to sell it.

While you are talking to book stores find out about readings and signings. This is part of your marketing plan information.

Libraries

Apply basically the same questions you've asked the book stores. You need to know if the libraries do buy self-published books.

Content and Design

It is now time to look closely at books. You have to decide what you want your book to look like. Do you want a big book, a small book, a fat book, or a thin book?

The following is a partial check-list:

Size
- Dimensions
- Paper weight

Cover
- Coated or laminated

Design
- Text design
- Photographs and art
- Binding — what kind?

Pricing
- Cost of production
- Cost of printing
- Cost of shipping
- Cost of fulfillment

If you have gone through this check list and are satisfied you want to continue, then we recommend you buy one of the books on self publishing and marketing. You are then in for the hard, but exciting work as an entrepreneur, self-publisher. Good luck.

Suggested books:

- *The Self-Publishing Manual* written and published by Dan Poynter, published by Para Publishing, Santa Barbara, California

- *Guerrilla Marketing for Writers* written by Jay Conrad Levinson, Rick Frishman & Michael Larsen published by Writer's Digest Books, Cincinnati, Ohio

Books and Bookmarks for Writers

By Marlene Howard,
Media Weavers/Writers Northwest Publisher

If you want to write and publish your work, read and become familiar with the following publications either in print or on the internet.

Print	Web
	Find libraries, quotations, www.libraryspot.com
Books in Print	www.booksinprint.com/bip/
Books Out of Print	www.abebooks.com

International Directory of Little
Magazines/Small Presses

Literary Agents of North America
Author Aid Associates
340 East 52 St
New York, NY 10022
P: 212-758-4213

A reference guide on both fee-charging and non-fee-charging literary agents, listing categories (poetry, fiction, and others), agency clients, subject interests, policies, ratio of works received to works placed and commissions.

The Insider's Guide to Book Editors, Publishers, and Literary Agents
Jeff Herman
Prima Publishing
P.O. Box 1260BK
Rocklin, CA 95677
P: 916-786-0426

A guide that provides the names and specialties of acquisition editors and literary agents, as well as how to get their attention.

Literary Marketplace	literarymarketplace.com
Publishers Weekly	publishersweekly.com

The following are websites that may be helpful to writers:

Search engines

Karnat   www.karnakcom

AskMe   www.askme.com

LookSmart   www.looksmart.com

Bookmarks

www.bookzonepro.com

www.bibliomania.com

www.compinfo-center.com/itmags.htm

www.backinprint.com

www.bibliocity.com

www.bookavenue.com

www.antiqubooks.com

www.alibris.com

www.poets.org

www.pw.org

www.poets.com

www.poem.com

www.poetrymagazine.com

www.poetrysociety.org

www.twc.org

www.potatohill.com

www.slate.com

www.salon.com

www.eb.com

www.levity.com/corduroy/index.htm

www.pbs.org

www.mindtools.com

www.refdesk.com

www.usgovinfo.about.com

www.pulitzer.org//index.html

www.westaf.org/about.php

www.fictionaddition.net

www.bookwire.com

www.aldaily.com

www.bartleby.com

www.creativecauldron.com

www.ticket2write.com

www.personalhistorians.org

www.nwu.org

www.sfwa.org

www.betweenthecovers.com/aw-ab/pul-lit.htm

Are You Ready to Become a Published Writer?

By Marlene Howard,
Media Weavers/Writers Northwest Publisher

You have studied and perfected your craft. You have written and re-written. You have edited, proofed and produced a manuscript you believe deserves to be printed. So take a deep breath, read the following advice and dive into the next phase of your writing career.

The old sales adage repeated often among sales people says, "nothing ever happens until somebody sells something." This applies to you the writer and your work. Your writing won't get published or read until you sell it.

Most writers are not sales people. Most of you would prefer not to struggle with marketing your work. However, since selling is part of becoming a professional writer it is important that you begin to understand the marketing process. This section has been developed to serve as a beginning marketing tool for sharing pertinent information and promoting communication and understanding among those who write and those who support the writing industry.

Regional publications may offer a better chance for beginning writers to find a market. For example, small local newspapers might be the place for you to sell an article or column. Many writers started this way and some have turned their columns into published books. Or, at least you can use those columns as clips to show an agent or editor that you are a published professional.

1. Know what you have to sell. Make it the most perfect manuscript, query letter or proposal you can produce. Polish it until each word sparkles. Edit and edit again, read it out loud to yourself or someone whose judgment you trust and then proofread and edit yet again.

2. Know your markets. Know who will want to read your work and who might be the best match to publish your work for your targeted readers. Find books that are similar to yours. I gave this advice to a novice writer recently and he assured me there are no books similar to his. Wrong. I took him to a bookstore and pointed out at least 20 books that any agent or editor would judge to be

similar to his. So, look around you. Go to the library and several bookstores. Each bookstore markets its offerings differently, especially the independents. Consider this important homework. Take notes on what is placed on front tables or displays. This clues you in on the kind of book the store staff likes to sell. This information will be valuable after your book is published. Even chain stores often feature regional books in a unique way.

3. Look for trends in publishing. There are not only trends in what is published, but there are trends in a book's appearance. Cover styles are fashion statements and change almost as often as clothing styles. Keep up. Know what you want your book to look like. What size do you picture it? You may not get to offer that input to your publisher, but it will help you sell your project if you have a positive, firm picture in your mind about what your book will ultimately look like.

4. Know your competition. Let me emphasize, "Writing is not a competitive sport and your writing will not be competing with what others have written." However, as a writer you must study the writing of others. If other books or articles similar to yours have been published recently, you will have to prove what is unique about your writing.

The Directory section of the Handbook can be only a beginning reference for you. Peruse the pages to learn the names of regional newspapers, magazines publishers. Next go to the library or bookstore to find examples of the publication or books they have produced. Study the publications, and then decide how your work could fit in with their offerings. If they have a website, look at it. If they offer guidelines send for them.

You are now prepared to go out and sell. Remember, rejection letters mean you are marketing. If you get even one or two hand written words on a rejection letter, that is a success story. It means you caught someone's attention. If they give you any suggestions, follow them and re-submit.

Keep trying, don't give up. And begin writing on the next project. If you've written a novel, vow to have the next novel at least 50% written by the time you sell the first one.

My writing mentor, Don James often closed his class with these words:

"READ, READ, READ — Read yourself full.
Then WRITE, WRITE, WRITE — Write yourself empty.
Your first million words is your apprenticeship."

For your convenience the Directory is divided into the following categories:

Organizations, Conferences and Networking
Contests
Residencies
Center for the Book Locations
Publishers

Also, continue to read the *Writers Northwest* Quarterly for updates and new opportunities.

Good Luck!

Writers Directory

Writers Organizations, Conferences and Networking Opportunities

Alaska

Homer
Kachemak Bay Writers' Conference, sponsored by Kachemak Bay Campus-Kenai Peninsula College-University of Alaska Anchorage. Held in Homer, Alaska this state-wide writing conference features over 35 workshops, craft talks and panel presentations in fiction, poetry, nonfiction, publishing, script writing, children's writing and nature writing.

Kachemak Bay Campus
Kenai Peninsula College
533 E. Pioneer Ave.
Homer, AK 99603
P: 907-235-7743
Web: chinook.kpc.alaska.edu/~conference/

Petersburg
Alaska Writers Workshop, sponsored by Petersburg Writers Guild, Alaska Council on the Arts, & Alaska Press Women.

Marilyn George
Box 1031
Petersburg, AK 99833
P: 907-772-4515

Idaho

Boise
The Log Cabin Literary Center is a nonprofit membership organization serving writers and readers with educational and cultural programs. Classes and workshops are offered for adults and emerging writers with resources for writers pursuing a publishing career. The Log Cabin conducts a Summer Writing Camp and places writers in Idaho schools to provide young people and teachers with innovative approaches to writing. Readings at the Log Cabin bring prominent authors to local

audiences. The fall Bookfest celebrates the written word with discussions, presentations and vendors.

Log Cabin Literary Center
801 S. Capitol Blvd., Suite 100
Boise, ID 83702
P: 208-331-8000
Web: www.logcablit.org/member.htm

Boise State University
The Writers and Readers Rendezvous features author readings, workshop sessions and book discussions. The Rendezvous is sponsored by the Boise State University Division of Extended Studies, Boise State University department of English, Idaho Humanities Council, Idaho Writers Connection and the Log Cabin Literary Center.
P: 426-1709 / 800-824-7017, ext. 1709
Web: news.boisestate.edu

Coeur d'Alene
Idaho Writers' League, Coeur d'Alene Chapter offers a Writers Fair that features authors, exhibitors, luncheon and networking. Topics include: autobiography/memoir, children's, nonfiction, religion/self help and science fiction/fantasy.

Mary L. Smith
1209 W. Woodlawn Dr.
Hayden, ID 83835-8812
Web: www.idahowritersleague.com/Coeur%20d%27Alene.html

Ketchum
The Sun Valley Writers' Conference and workshop, guided by a small board of directors, is an Idaho nonprofit organization with a volunteer Executive Director, a small group of consultants and energetic local volunteers. Anchored by important literary figures, the conference brings discerning readers and writers together in a congenial environment to consider ideas set forth in fiction, nonfiction, journalism, poetry and filmmaking.

SVWC
P.O. Box 957
Ketchum, ID 83340
P: 208-726-6670
Web: www.svwc.com

Lewisville

Snake River Rendezvous Writers Conference is a statewide nonprofit writers' organization with local chapters rotating as conference host.

Idaho Writers' League
467 N. 3200 E.
Lewisville, ID 83431-5019
Web: www.idahowritersleague.com

Montana

Big Timber

The Montana Cowboy Poetry Wintercamp is a celebration of western heritage, featuring all-day open-mike poetry, music and family entertainment. Nightrider Night Show features cowboy poets and musicians along with grassroots stories, poetry and music with plenty of humor.

Winter Camp
Box 1038
Big Timber, MT 59011
P: 932-4227

The Sagebrush Writers Workshop presents creative non-fiction and article writing. Advance manuscripts are accepted. Student readings and handouts included. In depth, personal instruction, writing exercises, examples and finding your "voice."

Sagebrush Writers Workshop
P.O. Box 1255
Big Timber, MT 59011-1255
P: 406-932-4227

Kalispell

Flathead River Writers Conference: Readings, workshops & one-on-one meetings with editor & agent for those qualified. Lodging available at conference site or nearby Located at the Grouse Mountain Lodge, Whitefish, in Northwest Montana, a few miles west of Glacier National

Park. Delta, Northwest, Horizon (Glacier Park Int'l Airport) and AMTRAK service the valley.

Jake How
Flathead River Writers Conference
P.O. Box 7711
Kalispell, MT 59904
E: hows@centurytel.net

Missoula

The Yellow Bay Writers' Workshop offers fiction, nonfiction, poetry workshops, readings, lectures, discussions and more.

Yellow Bay Writers' Workshop
The University of MT, Cont. Ed.
Missoula, MT 59812
P: 406-243-2094

Montana Festival of the Book features dozens of the region's writers in a variety of readings, panels, exhibits, demonstrations, a literary contest, signings, entertainment, receptions and satellite events. The Festival is presented by the Montana Center for the Book and the Montana Committee for the Humanities, in association with numerous national, state and local organizations and businesses.

Web: http://news.bookweb.org/mediaguide/672.html

Oregon

Ashland

National Writers Union — Ashland Writers meetings, last Monday monthly, 6:30 to 8 p.m., Gresham Room, Ashland Public Library.

Sharon McCann
E: mccann@mind.net.

Astoria

Monday Mike for Spoken Word — features readers and open mike, second Monday of each month, 7:30 p.m., River Coffee House & Theater, 230 W. Marine Drive, Astoria OR.

Florence Sage
E: sages@pacifier.com

Cannon Beach

Haystack Writing Classes take place at the Cannon Beach Elementary School, just south of Ecola Creek at 268 Beaver Street. The city of Cannon Beach is located on the Pacific Coast, 80 miles west of Portland and can be reached by Highways 26 and 101.

PSU Summer Session
P.O. Box 1491
Portland OR 97207-1491
P: 503-725-4832 / 800-547-8887 ext 4832.

Eugene

Lane Literary Guild (LLG)
44 W. Broadway, #304
Eugene, OR 97401
P: 541-683-4985
E: calendar@laneliteraryguild.org
Web: www.laneliteraryguild.org.

Writers Roundtable second Wednesday monthly, 4 to 6 p.m.

Tsunami Books
National Writers Union (NWU)
Oregon Local
2585 Willamette Blvd.
P.O. Box 10821
Eugene, OR 97440
P: 877-797-4837
Web: www.oregonwriters.org
Web: www.nwu.org

General meetings the first Thursday monthly, 6:30 to 8:30 p.m. Free to WW members; $5 non-members.

Willamette Writers Mid-Valley Chapter
Hilyard Street Community Center
2580 Hilyard Street
Eugene, OR
E: wilwrite@willamettewriters.com.

Medford

General meetings first Saturday monthly, 10 a.m. to noon. Free to WW members, $5 non-members.

Willamette Writers Southern Oregon Chapter
226 E. Main St.
Medford, OR.
P: 541-955-9365.

Newport

Nye Beach Writers Series hosts events third Saturday monthly, 7 p.m., followed by open mike for 5-minute readings by audience members. General admission $7; members of Oregon Coast Council for the Arts $6.

Nye Beach Writers Series
Studio Theatre
Performing Arts Center
777 West Olive St.
Newport, OR 97365
Web: www.coastarts.org/writers
P: 541-574-7708
E: cperry@pioneer.net

Noti

Society of Children's Book Writers and Illustrators
Oregon Chapter
P.O. Box 336
Noti, OR 97461
P: 541-935-4589
Web: users.rio.com/robink/scbwi.html
Web: www.scbwi.org

Portland

"Bloody Thursday" meetings, free, open to the public, last Thursday monthly from September to May, 7:30 p.m. with social hour at 7 p.m. at the NW Neighborhood Cultural Center, 1819 NW Everett St., Portland, OR.

Friends of Mystery
P.O. Box 8251
Portland, OR 97207
P: 503-241-0759
E:info@friendsofmystery.org
Web: www.friendsofmystery.org

Left Coast Crime
P.O. Box 18033
Portland, OR, 97218-0033
P: 503-281-9449
E: wrigcros@teleport.com
Web: www.spiritone.com/jlorentz/leftcoast

Oregon Writers Colony is an organization of writers who offer spring and fall conferences, opportunities to stay at the coastal retreat house, The Colonyhouse, an annual conference and bi-monthly presentations by writers and publishers.

Oregon Writers Colony
P.O. Box 15200
Portland OR, 97293-5200
P: 503-827-8072
Web: www.oregonwriterscolony.org

Sisters in Crime-Harriet Vane Chapter, Monthly programs for mystery writers and readers, third Monday monthly.

Sisters in Crime
P.O. Box 2458
Portland, OR 97208-2458
Web: www.sinc-in.org

Society for Technical Communication
Willamette Valley Chapter
P: 503-242-1169
Web: www.stcwvc.org.

Willamette Writers holds monthly meetings on the first Tuesdays. Sponsors annual conference in August.

Willamette Writers
9045 SW Barbur Blvd., Ste. 5A
Portland OR 97219-4027
P: 503-452-1592
E: wilwrite@willamettewriters.com

West Linn
Oregon State Poetry Association
P.O. Box 602
West Linn, OR 97068
E: ospa@teleport.com
Web: www.oregonpoets.org.

Winchester
The Association of Writers is open to all writers in the Douglas County area, published and unpublished, and hosts monthly meetings with speakers.

Association of Writers
P.O. Box 1101
Winchester, OR 97495
E: sybilla@rosenet.net.

Washington

Bellevue
The Publishing Institute
Bellevue Community College
3000 Landerholm Circle SE
Bellevue, WA 98007-6484

P: 425-564-2943
E: gcampbel@bcc.ctc.edu

Bothell
Sundial Press provides researching, writing, editing, graphics, and layout services.

Sundial Press LLC
P.O. Box 401
Bothell, WA 98011

P: 425-821-2411
E: gcampb2965@aol.com

Bremerton
First Friday Reading Series, first Friday monthly, 6 p.m., at Just Your Cup O'Tea, 305 Pacific Avenue (four blocks from ferry dock). Features three readers and open mike.

E: svend@sinclair.net.

Edmonds

Pacific Northwest Writers Association is one of the oldest writing organization in Washington. They sponsor an annual July writers' conference in the Seattle area.

Pacific Northwest Writers Association
P.O. Box 2016
Edmonds, WA 98020-9516
P: 425-673-2665
Web: www.pnwa.org

Issaquah

Four Poets and an Open Mike, second Sunday monthly, 3 to 4:30 p.m. features four readers and an open mike at Barnes and Noble Booksellers, 1530 11 Ave. NW, Issaquah, WA.

Langley

The Whidbey Island Writers' Association is a group of volunteers dedicated to offering support to writers through quality services, and educational and networking opportunities.

Whidbey Island Writers' Association
P. O. Box 1289
WA 98260
E: writers@whidbey.com

Olympia

Olympia Poetry Network, poetry readings 6:30 p.m., third Wednesday monthly, Traditions Fair Trade Café, 5th and Water Streets, Olympia, WA.

E: cdahl151@aol.com
Web: www.thurston.com/~yake/opn.html.

Port Angeles

Foothills Writers Series
Peninsula College
1502 E. Lauridsen Blvd
Port Angeles, WA 98362.

Seattle

Clarion West is an intensive six-week workshop for writers preparing for professional careers in science fiction and fantasy, held annually at Seattle Central Community College in Seattle, Wash.

Clarion West
340 Fifteenth Ave. East, Suite 350
Seattle WA 98112
P: 206-322-9083

It's About Time Writers, second Thursday monthly, 6:30 to 8:30 p.m. features four readers and an open mike at the Seattle Public Library, 5009 Roosevelt Way NE, Seattle, WA

PoetsWest at the Frye, Frye Art Museum, 704 Terry Ave. Seattle, WA.

PoetsWest
1011 Boren Ave.
PMB 155
Seattle, WA 98104
P: 206-682-1268
E: info@poetswest.com.

Northwest Bookfest is a two-day event for a region that's crazy about books, reading and writing. Over the past seven years, Bookfest has become the Pacific Northwest's largest and most anticipated gathering of bookworms, with over 250 authors, 200 exhibitor booths, the Northwest's largest book arts exhibition, and more than 25,000 visitors.

Northwest Bookfest
P.O. Box 28129
Seattle, WA 98118
P: 206-378-1883
E: info@nwbookfest.org

Red Sky Poetry Theatre
Globe Café and Bakery
1531 14th
Seattle, WA
P: 206-324-8815.

Richard Hugo House, whose mission is to build a vital learning community that develops and sustains practicing writers doing essential work. It is a place that nurtures writers, readers and audiences of books, plays, films, and brings innovative and effective writing. Richard Hugo House runs a variety of programs for writers and the local community.

Richard Hugo House
1634 Eleventh Ave.
Seattle WA 98122
P: 206-322-7030
E: welcome@hugohouse.org
Web: www.hugohouse.org.

Seattle Free Lances, an association of published writers meets first Tuesday monthly, September to June, 5:30 p.m. no-host social hour followed by no-host dinner at Rock Salt Steak House on Lake Union, 1232 Westlake Ave., Seattle, WA. After-dinner program features guest speakers or panel discussions. Members welcome to bring guests.

P: 425-743-0254.

University Book Store offers free readings in General Book Department.

University Book Store
4326 University Way NE
Seattle, WA 98105
P: 206-634-3400 / 800-355-READ
Web: www.ubookstore.com

University of Washington
UW Extension
5001 25th Ave. NE
Seattle, WA 98105-4190. 206-543-2310 / 800-543-2430
Web: www.extension.washington.edu.

Tacoma
Poetry readings, second Tuesday monthly, at 7 p.m., Kickstand Café, Fawcett and 6th, Tacoma, WA.

P: 253-383-3311

Puget Sound Poetry Connection, Distinguished Writers Series, second Friday monthly, 7 p.m. at Sleep and Story, 1936 Pacific Ave., Tacoma, WA.

Vancouver
NW Poetry Coalition Open Mike Poetry Group, second Wednesday monthly, 7-8:30 p.m., at the Library Hall, Vancouver Community Library, Vancouver, WA.

E: ckidder@hotmail.com.

Woodinville
Poetry Night in Woodinville with Open Mike, last Wednesday monthly, 7-9 p.m. features three readers and open mike at Barnes & Noble Booksellers, 18025 Garden Way NE, Woodinville, WA.

Other Locations

BrightSide BookWorks
2605 E. Serendipity Circle #151F
Colorado Springs, CO 80917
P: 719-597-8587
E: brightsidebookworks@yahoo.com

Women Writing the West
8547 E. Arapahoe Rd,#J-541
Greenwood Village, CO 80112-1436
P: 303-690-6038

A nonprofit organization that publishes an annual catalog of its members and provides educational and industry information to the membership and to the publishing community.

Contests and Literary Awards

Alaska

The John Haines Award for Poetry: $500 plus publication in the Winter Solstice Issue of *ICE-FLOE: International Poetry of the Far North*. Send one poem with $20 fee (includes annual subscription to ICE-FLOE).

Ice-Floe Press, John Haines Award
P.O. Box 92878
Anchorage, AK 99509-2878.
Web: www.icefloepress.com for more information.

Idaho

Annual Literary Award recognizes and honors one book, selected from among all the books published in any one calendar year, which has made an outstanding contribution to the body of printed materials about Idaho. The award is intended to encourage the writing and publishing of books about Idaho, and to encourage excellence in writing and high standards of accuracy and readability in those books.

Elaine Watson, Idaho Book Award
Albertsons Library, Boise State University
1910 University Drive
Boise, ID 83725-1430
P: 208-426-1737
E: ewatson@boisestate.edu

Oregon

Annual Poetry Contest, by Portland Branch, National League of American Pen Women. Any style, subject, 40 lines maximum. Prizes: $150, $50, $25, Honorable Mention(s). Fee: $3 per poem, include SASE for guidelines.

NLAPW, Portland Branch
c/o Joan P. Henson
6071 SW Prosperity Rd.
Tualatin, OR 97062
P: 503-638-7488

Oregon Writers Colony Annual Writing Contest. Prizes: first place $200, second place $100, third place $50. Generally the same rules apply each year.

Nancy Boutin, OWC Writing Contest
P.O. Box 15200
Portland OR 97293-5200
P: 503-827-8072
Web: oregonwriterscolony.org

Glimmer Train competitions: Short story award for new writers, VERY SHORT Fiction Award (Sample copy: $9.95) You can now make your submissions online.

Web: www.glimmertrain.com

Oregon Book Awards presented annually by Literary Arts to Oregon writers who work in genres of poetry, fiction, literary nonfiction, drama and young readers literature. The five Oregon Book Awards, each in the amount of $1,000, are available for work published or produced in the following genres: Poetry — including chapbooks of more than 20 pages in length; Fiction — including novels, novellas, and collected short stories of more than 20 pages in length; Literary Nonfiction — including biography, autobiography, memoir, collected essays, history, natural history, landscape writing and criticism. The work must be predominantly text (not purely informational or strictly factual) and not primarily photography or art; Drama — including one-act plays, radio and television plays, and one-person productions; and Young Readers Literature — including poetry, fiction and nonfiction. Work must be written by a current full-time and living Oregon resident. Exception: A qualified resident who dies after his or her book is submitted may receive a posthumous award.

Literary Arts, Inc.
219 NW 12th Avenue, Suite 201
Portland, OR 97209
P: 503-227-2583
Web: www.literary-arts.org/wis.html

Willamette Writers Annual Awards: Kay Snow Writing Awards are named for the founder of Willamette Writers. The annual contest awards include one first prize of $300, one second place prize of $150 and a third place prize of $50 per winning entry in each of the six categories; fiction, nonfiction, juvenile, poetry, student writer and screenwriting. Student writers are awarded $50 for first place in three grade divisions. The Liam Callen Memorial Award of $500 goes to the best overall contest entry in all divisions

Willamette Writers
9045 S.W. Barbur Blvd., Suite 5A
Portland, OR 97219-4027
P: 503-452-1592
Web: www.willamettewriters.com

Washington

Pacific Northwest Writers Association Annual Writing Contest includes first, second and third place prizes in the following categories: Poetry, Screenwriting, Adult Short Story, Adult Genre Novel, Adult Non-genre Novel, Juvenile/Young Adult Novel, Non-fiction Book or Memoir, Adult Article, Essay or Short Memoir Juvenile Short Story or Picture Book.

Pacific Northwest Writers Association
P.O. Box 2016
Edmonds, WA 98020-9516
P: 425-673-2665
Web: www.pnwa.org

Washington State Book Awards are presented at the annual awards ceremony in the fall. The honored works are selected by a jury for literary merit, lasting importance and overall quality of the publication. There are no categories for the awards (e.g., more than one or no poetry books may be selected in a given year). A Washington author is a writer who meets at least one of the following criteria: (1) was born in Washington State; (2) spent at least 10 of the first 18 years of his/her life in Washington; or (3) is a current resident of Washington and the work was published after at least one year of residency in the state.

Nancy Pearl, Executive Director
Washington Center for the Book at the Seattle Public Library
P: 206-386-4184
or
Chris Higashi, Associate Director
Washington Center for the Book at the Seattle Public Library
P: 206-386-4650
Web: www.humanities.org/awards/gwa.html

Residencies

Montana

Montana Artists Refuge

The Montana Artists Refuge, located in Basin, Mont., is organized to further the creative work of artists, to create residencies for artists, and to provide arts programs and arts education for both artists and community members. The Refuge hosts short and long-term residencies where artists can pursue new interests, finish projects, or relax and feel inspired by the landscape. Contact with local artists provides residents with opportunities for interaction and creative collaboration.

Montana Artists Refuge
P.O. Box 8
Basin, MT 59631
P: (406) 225-3500
E: mar@mt.net

Oregon

Caldera Residency Fellowships

Caldera Residency Fellowships are for artists and writers at five A-frame cottages on a 90-acre site on Blue Lake in the Deschutes National Forest, 17 miles west of Sisters, Ore. Applicants are required to submit examples of work created in last three years. Member of Alliance of Artists' Communities.

Miriam Feuerle, Director of Adult Programs
224 NW 13th Ave.
Portland, OR 97209
P: 503-937-7563
F: 503-937-8563
E: miriam.feuerle@wk.com

For residencies throughout the world:
Web: www.artistcommunities.org

Oregon Writers Colony

The Oregon Writers Colonyhouse is a writer's haven located in Rockaway Beach, Ore., overlooking the Pacific Ocean to the west and Lake Lytle to the east. It is a special place to go to write; owned and managed by writers, for writers. Available to all Oregon Writers Colony members on a first come, first serve basis with special low winter and weekday rates.

Oregon Writers Colony
P.O. Box 15200
Portland OR 97293-5200
P: 503-827-8072
Web: oregonwriterscolony.org

Fishtrap: Imnaha Writers' Retreat

Fishtrap's Imnaha Writers' Retreat is a quiet time and place for a handful of writers to write. Housing and meals are provided at a private lodge on the wild and scenic Imnaha River in northeast Oregon. Participants have days free to write, read, enjoy the natural beauty of this remote area and take evening meals together. Fishtrap alumni are invited to apply for two to four week sessions during spring and fall.

Fishtrap, Inc.
P.O. Box 38
Enterprise, OR 97328
P: 541-426-3623
F: 541-426-9075

Sitka Center for Art & Ecology

A writers-in-residence program is offered for writers, artists, naturalists who have a degree or professional experience. Length: 3-9 months. Facilities: 1,500 square-foot main workspace plus additional studios; self-contained lodging facilities, along Oregon's central coast.

Sitka Center for Art & Ecology
P.O. Box 65
Otis, OR 97368
P: 503-994-5485

Soapstone: A Writing Retreat for Women

Soapstone is located in the Oregon Coast Range. Its residency program was created to serve the needs of women writers working on fiction, poetry, drama and other literary writing. Send an SASE.

Soapstone
622 SE 29th Avenue
Portland, OR 97214
E: mail@soapstone.org
Web: www.soapstone.org.

Walden Farm

The residency at Walden Farm includes a fully furnished cabin with space for one working writer. Sponsored by a private citizen and coordinated by Extended Campus Programs at Southern Oregon University, the Walden residency fellowship program seeks to encourage Oregon writers of fiction, poetry, plays and creative non-fiction with the opportunity to pursue their work at a quiet and beautiful mountain farm in southern Oregon. Three residencies during spring and summer are awarded each year. Applicants must be Oregon residents and must agree upon acceptance, not to smoke, to do their own cooking, and to keep the cabin in good order.

Brooke Friendly, Coordinator
Southern Oregon University
Extended Campus Programs
1250 Siskiyou Blvd.
Ashland, OR 97520
P: 541-552-6901
F: 541-552-6047

Washington

Centrum Artist Residencies

Centrum hosts an annual writers' conference and residency programs.

Centrum
P.O. Box 1158
Port Townsend, WA 98368-0958
P: 360-385-3102
F: 360-385-2470
Web: www.centrum.org

Hedgebrook

Overlooking Puget Sound on Whidbey Island in Washington, Hedgebrook is a privately funded, not-for-profit artists' community for women writers of all ages and from all cultural backgrounds. Write for residence, application, stipend, and/or travel assistance information. Send a self-addressed, first-class stamped #10 envelope.

Hedgebrook
2197 E. Millman Rd.
Langley, WA 98260
Web: www.hedgebrook.org/pages/home.html

Willard R. Espy Literary Foundation

The Foundation's Writer's Residency Program provides one-month residencies in the quiet village of Oysterville on Willapa Bay in southwest Washington. Applications can be downloaded from the Foundation website.

Willard R. Espy Literary Foundation
P.O. Box 614
Oysterville, WA 98641
P: 360-665-5220
F: 360-665-5224
E: wrelf@willapabay.org
Web: www.espyfoundation.org

Center for the Book
Locations in the Northwest

Alaska Center for the Book
Loussac Library
3600 Denali St.
Anchorage, AK 99503-6093
P: 907-278-8838 / F: 907-278-8839
E: akctrbk@akcenter.com
Web: www.alaskacenterforthebook.org

Idaho Center for the Book
Boise State University
1910 University Dr.
Boise, ID 83725
P: 208-426-1999 / F: 208-426-4373
Web: www.lili.org/icb

Montana Center for the Book
311 Brantly Hall
The University of Montana
Missoula, MT 59812-8214
P: 406-243-6022 / 800-624-6001 / F: 406-243-4836
Web: www.montanabook.org

Oregon Center for the Book
Oregon State Library Bldg.
250 Winter St. NE
Salem, OR 97310-0640
P: 503-378-2112, ext. 239
Web: www.osl.state.or.us/home/libdev/CFTBoverview.html

Washington Center for the Book
Seattle Public Library
800 Pike St.
Seattle, WA 98101
P: 206-386-4184 / F: 206-386-4119
Web: www.spl.lib.wa.us/wacentbook/centbook.html

"Nine out of ten writers, I am sure, could write more.

I think they should and, if they did,

they would find their work improving

even beyond their own, their agent's and

their editor's highest hopes."

John Creasey

Publishers

Alaska Book Publishers

Alaska Angler & Alaskan Hunter Publications
Chris Batin
P.O. Box 83550
Fairbanks, AK 99708
P: 907-455-8000
E: chrisbatin@alaskaangler.com
Web: www.alaskaangler.com

Fishing and hunting reports, advice and how-to books.

Alaska Geographic Society
P.O. Box 93370
Anchorage, AK 99509-3370
P: 907-562-0164
F: 907-562-0579
E: akgeo@akgeo.com
Web: www.akgeo.com

Alaska Geographic Books on all aspects of Alaska and the North, including its people, resources, animals, regions geographic features and more. Mailed to members, subscribers and sold in bookstores

Alaska Natural History Association
750 W. Second Ave. #100
Anchorage, AK 99501
P: 907-274-8440
F: 907-274-8343
Web: www.alaskanha.org

Books, maps, guides, posters and other information about Alaska's parks, forests and refuges. Dedicated to enhancing understanding and conservation of the natural, cultural and historical resources of Alaska'a public lands.

University Of Alaska Museum
907 Yukon Dr.
Fairbanks, AK 99775
P: 907-474-6939
Web: www.fairbanks-alaska.com

Soft cover books and newsletter. Query w/SASE. Catalog i
s available.

Denali Press
P.O. Box 021535
Juneau, AK 99802-1535
P: 907-586-6014
Web: www.denalipress.com

Softcover originals — nonfiction and biographies. Prefer primarily reference books, but will also publsih travel guides, Alaskana and cultural diversity. Query w/clips, sample chapters, outline, synopsis. Catalog available.

Paws Iv Publishing Co.
P.O. Box 2364
Homer, AK 99603

P: 907-235-7697

Softcover nonfiction and fiction on Alaska, children/teen stories, adventure. Query w/SASE.

Salmon Run Press
John Smelcher
P.O. Box 231081
Anchorage, AK 99523
P: 907-337-4585

Children's, nature, Native American and poetry. Query first with SASE.

University Of Alaska Press
P.O. Box 756240
Fairbanks, AK 99775
P: 907-474-5831
F: 907-474-5502
E: fypress@uaf.edu
Web: www.uaf.edu/uapress

Publishes works of scholarship that will increase the store of knowledge about Alaska and the North. Alaska politics and history, Native languages and culture, education, biographies and scientific topics.

Winterholm Press
P.O. Box 101251
Anchorage, AK 99510

Self publisher of Alaska fishing books.

Wolfdog Publications
P.O. Box 142506, Dept. R
Anchorage, AK 99514

Dog Sledding Books

Alaska Northwest Books
203 W. 15th Ave.
Anchorage, AK 99501
P: 907-278-8838
Web: www.alaskaone.com/aknwbook

Alaska Pocket Guides, books on wildlife, Denali cookbooks.

Alaska Outdoor Adventures
Whittier, AK 99693
P: 907-472-2392

Prints guides for Alaskan vacation needs.

Earthpulse Press
Eagle River, AK 99577
P: 907-249-9111
F: 907-696-1277
E: info@earthpulse.com
Web: www.earthpulse.com

Frontier science and politics. Reporting on matters which are not covered by the mainstream media.

Misty Mountain Publishing
Anchorage, AK 99501
P: 907-258-9800

Children's books

Prince William Sound Books
P.O. Box 1313
Valdez, AK 99686
P: 907-835-5175
E: pwsbooks@cvinternet.net

Fiction, drama, poetry, history, Observer Guides, Cruising Guides

Todd Communications
203 W. 15th Ave.
Anchorage, AK 99508
P: 907-274-8633:
Alaska Photographs

Turnagain Press
Anchorage, AK 99501
P: 907-248-6806 :
Advice books

University of Alaska Press
P.O. Box 756240
Eielson rm. 104, UAF Campus
Fairbanks, AK 99775-6240
P: 907-474-5831
F: 907-474-5502
E: orders.uapress@uaf.edu
Web: www.uaf.edu/uapress

Travel; Nature/Environ-
ment;Other: circumpolar
regions

Williwaw Publishing Co.
P.O. Box 14288
Anchorage, AK 99514
P: 907-338-8883
F: 907-333-9506
E: info@williwaw.com
Web: www.williwaw.com

Alaska weather calendar
(photos), Alaska non-fiction —
science, natural history, history.
Query by mail or email.

Alaska Periodicals

Alaska Business Monthly
501 W. Northern Lights Blvd.,
Ste. 2100
Anchorage, AK 99503-2577

P: 907-276-4373
Web: www.akbizmag.com
Business magazine.

Alaska History
P.O. Box 100299
Anchorage, AK 99510-0299
P: 907-276-1596
E: ahs@alaska.net
Soft cover journals.

Alaska Historical Society
Alaska Medicine
4107 Laurel St.
Anchorage, AK 99508
P: 907-562-0304
E: asma@alaska.net
Web: www.akmed.org

Alaska Quarterly Review
U OF AK
3211 Providence Dr.
Anchorage, AK 99508

A journal devoted to
contemporary literary art.

Alaskan Byways
P.O. Box 211356
Anchorage, AK 99521

We Alaskans
1001 Northway Dr.
Anchorage, AK 99514-9001
P: 907-257-4318

Mushing
P.O. Box 149
Ester, AK 99725-0149
P: 907-479-0454
E: editor@mushing.com
Web: www.mushing.com

Alaska Angler Publications
P.O. Box 83550
Fairbanks, AK 99708
P: 907-455-8000
E: chrisbatin@alaskaangler.com
Web: www.alaskaangler.com

Alaska Branching Out
193 Arctic Health Bldg.
Fairbanks, AK 99775-5200
P: 907-474-6356
F: 907-474-7439

Forestry in Alaska

New River Times
201 1st Ave.
Fairbanks, AK 99701-4848

Periodical.

Southeastern Log
P.O. Box 7900
Ketchikan, AK 99901
P: 907-225-3157

Northwest Arctic NUNA
P.O. BOX 256
Kotzebue, AK 99752
P: 907-442-3311

Adventures
Sheldon Jackson College
Sitka, AK 99835

Alaska Horse Journal
310 N. Harriette St.
Wasilla, AK 99654-7627
P: 907-376-4470
E: akhorse@corecom.net

Alask Horse Journal, the only
monthly equestrian magazine
published in Alaska.

Alaska Newspapers

Anchorage Daily News
1001 Northway Dr.
Anchorage, AK 99508-2098
P: 907-257-4200
Web: www.adn.com

Chugiak/Eagle River Star
16941 N. Eagle River Loop Rd.
Eagle River, AK 99577-7499
P: 907-694-2727
F: 907-694-1545
Web: www.alaskastar.com

Delta Wind
2887 Alaska Hwy
Delta Junction, AK 99737
P: 907-895-5515

Fairbanks Daily News-Miner
200 N. Cushman St.
Fairbanks, AK 99701-2832
P: 907-452-5054
Web: www.news-miner.com

Homer News
3482 Landing St.
Homer, AK 99603-7999
P: 907-235-7767
Web: www.homeralaska.com

Juneau Empire
3100 Channel Dr.
Juneau, AK 99801-7814
P: 907-586-3740
Web: www.juneauempire.com

Ketchikan Daily News
501 Dock St.
Ketchikan, AK 99901
P: 907-225-3157

Kodiak Daily Mirror
1419 Selig St.
Kodiak, AK 99615-6450
P: 907-486-3227
Web:
www.ptialaska.net/~kdmnews

Petersburg Pilot
P.O. Box 930
Petersburg, AK 99833
P: 907-772-9393
Web: www.petersburgpilot.com

The Cordova Times
P.O. Box 200
Cordova, AK 99574-0200
P: 907-424-7181

The Daily Sitka Sentinel
P.O. Box 799
Sitka, AK 99835
P: 907-747-3219

The Nome Nugget
P.O. Box 610
Nome, AK 99762
P: 907-443-5235
Web: www.nomenuget.com

The Peninsula Clarion
150 Trading Bay Rd, Ste. 1
Kenai, AK 99611
P: 907-283-7551
Web: www.peninsulaclarion.com

Valdez Vanguard
337 Fairbanks Dr
Valdez, AK 99686
P: 907-835-2211

Wrangell Sentinel
P.O. Box 798
Wrangell, AK 99929
P: 907-874-2301

Idaho Book Publishers

ABC Feelings, Inc. / Adage Publications
P.O. Box 2377
Coeur d'Alene, ID 83816-2377
P: 208-762-3177
F: 208-762-3177
E: feelings@iea.com
Web: www.home-school/mail/
abcfeelings.html

Backeddy Books
P.O. Box 301
Cambridge, ID 83610
P: 208-257-3810
Old West

Boise Front Adventures, Inc.
Boise, ID 83702
P: 208-345-4802
Travel and adventure in Idaho.

Boise State University Western Writers Series
1910 University Ave.
Boise, ID 83725
P: 208-426-3041
E: tpenry@boisestate.edu
Booklets to deepen the understanding and appreciation of the American West. Of 150 published titles, the majority focus on the life and work of individual writers sho have made significant contributions to western American literature

Caldera Publishing
P.O. Box 111
Pocatello, ID 93204-0111
P: 208-234-1159
E: redmeyers@aol.com

Canon Press
205 E. 5th St.
Moscow, ID 83843
P: 208-883-8932
Web: www.canonpress.org
Small publishing ministry of Christ Church, Moscow, Idaho. Dedicated to providing "select literature for growing in the Chrisitian faith."

Caxton Press
312 Main St.
Caldwell, ID 83605
P: 208-459-7421
F: 208-459-7450
E: sgipson@caxtonprinters.com
Web: www.caxtonprinters.com
Nonfiction hard and soft cover original books on history, travel, biography, lifestyle, western Americana. Query with outline, sample chapters, SASE.

Confluence Press/Lewis-Clark State College
8th Ave. & 6th St.
Lewiston, ID 83501
P: 208-799-2336
F: 208-799-2850
Web: www.confluencepress.com
trade books of poetry, fiction, novels, history, essays, literary criticism, photography, art, science and folklore. Special interest in the literature of the contemporary American West. NO EMAIL QUERIES.

Griffith Publishing

P.O. Box 247
Caldwell, ID 83606
P: 208-454-9553
F: 208-454-1045
E: jlg@primenet.com
Web: www.hodi.com

Business and health books for businesses, organizations and self-publishing authors.

Healthwise, Inc.

2601 Bogus Basin Rd.
Boise, ID 83702
P: 208-345-1161
F: 208-345-1897
E: bfoster@healthwise.org
Web: www.healthwise.org

Publishes health care info aimed at better informing patients. Prescription-Strength Information™.

Hemingway Western Studies Series – Boise State University

1910 University Dr.
Boise, ID 83725
P: 208-385-1999
E: ttrusky@boisestate.edu

Books relating to Intermountain West, its cultures, the environment, politics, arts, social issues and history. Query with outline, SASE.

Idaho State Historical Society

450 N. 4th St.
Boise, ID 83702
P: 208-334-3428

Idaho history nonfiction, biography and memoirs. Query

with outline or synopsis and sample chapters. SASE.

Keokee Co. Publishing

Chris Bessler
P.O. Box 722
Sandpoint, ID 83864
P: 208-263-3573
F: 208-263-4045
E: info@keokee.com
Web: www.keokee.com

Publishes under its own imprint or on contract.

Legendry Publishing Co.

P.O. Box 7706
Boise, ID 83707
P: 208-376-9814

U.S. History, family, health. Query

Marsh Creek Press

P.O. Box 700
Pocatello, ID 83201
P: 208-232-6316
F: 208-232-6286
E: tobih@aol.com
Web: www.donaslett.com/marshcreek.html

Mountain Meadow Press

HC 75, Box 13
Koosie, ID 83539
P: 208-926-7875
Web: www.mountainmeadowpressonline.com

Lewis & Clark Expedition Journals, books on Sacagawea, Nez Perce Indians, Idaho history and travel.

**Pacific Press
Publishing Association**
Seventh-Day Adventist Church
1350 N. Kings Rd.
Nampa, ID 83687
P: 208-465-2500
Religion. Query w/SASE.

Polecat Press
612 West Haycraft
Coeur d'Alene, ID 83815
P: 888-776-5427
F: 208-664-4248
Web: www.communication
designs.com/polecat/
index.html
Don Hoskins' books

Powder Mountain Press
189 N. Main Street
Driggs, ID 83422
P: 208-354-3466
F: 208-354-3468
E: powdermtn@tetonmags.com
Web: www.tetonmags.com
Books and magazines about
the Grand Tetons and
surrounding area.

Silver Creek Press, Inc.
P.O. Box 4457
Hailey, ID 83333
P: 208-788-2210
F: 208-788-8648
E: email@silvercreekpress.net
Web: www.silvercreekpress.net
Flyfishing and wildlife calendars,
magazines and books. Offers
editorial creation, advertising,
design, layout, printing and
overall strategic project
management.

Tamarack Books
P.O. Box 190313
Boise, ID 83719
P: 208-387-2650
U.S. History, travel, old west.
Query w/SASE

Treasure Valley Publishing
Rhonda L. Johnson
1121 N. Meridan St.
Meridian, ID 83642
P: 208-288-0453
E: nrjo@qwest.net
Web: www.treasurevalley
publishing.com
Booklets, books, pamphlets
educational and math related.
Also provides Shiloh
Educational Resources.

University Of Idaho Press
The University of Idaho,
Moscow, ID 83843
P: 208-885-7564
Major genre published by the
Press include folklore, Western
American literature, Native
American studies, natural
history, resource and policy
studies, and regional histories
and studies. Original, reprint,
subsidy books. Hard and soft
cover. Query w/outline, sample
chapters and SASE.

Idaho Periodicals

Northwest Journal
112 W. 4th
Moscow, ID 83843
P: 208-882-6704

Our Little Friend
P.O. Box 7000
Boise, ID 83707
Weekly magazine for children
published by Seventh-Day
Adventist Church.

Outdoor Digest
P.O. Box 1944
Twin Falls, ID 83303-1944

Owyhee Outpost
P.O. BOX 67
Murphy, ID 83650
P: 208-495-2319

Peak Media, Inc.
P.O. Box 925
Hailey, ID 83333-0925
P: 208-726-9494
Publishes magazines with a
focus on the region.

Potato Grower of Idaho
P.O. Box 949
Blackfoot, ID 83221
Monthly.

Potlatch Times
P.O. BOX 1016
Lewiston, ID 83501
Monthly for employees and
business community.

Quest for Excellence
190 E. Bannock
Boise, ID 83712
Quarterly magazine for patients,
staff and friends of the hospital.

Rancher-Stockman-Farmer
P.O. Box 714
Meridian, ID 83642
P: 208-888-1165
Quarterly newspaper.

R.N. Idaho
200 N. 4th St., Ste. 20
Boise, ID 83702-6001

Smoke Signals
1350 Kings Road
Nampa, ID 83651
Monthly of the Seventh-Day
Adventist Church.

**Snake River Alliance
Newsletter**
P.O. Box 1731
Boise, ID 83701
P: 208-344-9161

Sugar Producer
520 Park Ave
Idaho Falls, ID 83402
P: 208-524-7000

The Advocate
P.O. Box 895
Boise, ID 83701
P: 208-342-8958
Idaho state bar.

The Flyfisher
P.O. Box 1387
Idaho Falls, ID 83403-1387
P: 208-523-7300

Quarterly journal of the
Federation of Fly Fishers.

Timberline
6150 Indian Tree Lane
Pocatello, ID 83204
P: 208-236-2470

Literary magazine.

**Upper Snake River Valley
Historical Society**
P.O. Box 244
Rexburg, ID 83440
P: 208-356-9101

Valley Magazine
P.O. Box 925
Hailey, ID 83333
P: 208-788-4500

Adopted Child
P.O. Box 9362
Moscow, ID 83843
P: 208-882-1181

Appaloosa Journal
2720 W. Pullman Rd.
Moscow, ID 83843
P: 208-882-5578
208-882-8150
E: journal@appaloosa.com
Web: www.appaloosa.com

Boise Business Today
P.O. Box 2368
Boise, ID 83701

Dairyline
1365 N. Orchard
Boise, ID 83760

Bimonthly.

Em-Kayan
P.O. BOX 73
Boise, ID 83707

Farm & Ranch Chronicle
P.O. Box 157
Cottonwood, ID 83522
P: 208-962-3851

Farm Journal Magazine
S. 2517 Greenferry Rd.
Coeur d'Alene, ID 83814
P: 208-664-9324

Idaho Yesterdays
450 N. 4th St.
Boise, ID 83702-6027
P: 208-334-3428
208-334-3198
Web: www.idahohistory.net

Idaho history.

Line Rider
2120 Airport Way
Boise, ID 83705-5197

Cattlemans association
quarterly.

Boise Family Magazine
13191 W. Scotfield St.
Boise, ID 83713-0889
P: 208-938-2119
F: 208-938-2117
Web: www.boisefamily.com

A magazine for parenting.

Shoot! Magazine
1770 W. State St., Ste. 340
Boise, ID 83702
P: 208-368-9920
F: 208-338-8428
Web: www.shootmagazine.com
Western action-shooting and the
old west.

Idaho Newspapers

Bonner County Daily Bee
P.O. Box 159
Sandpoint, ID 83864-1345
P: 208-263-9534
Web: www.bonnercountydaily
bee.com

Clearwater Tribune
P.O. Box 71
Orofino, ID 83544-0071
P: 208-476-4571
F: 208-476-0765
Web: www.clearwater
tribune.com

Coeur d'Alene Press
P.O. Box 7000
Coeur d'Alene, ID 83814
P: 208-664-8176
F: 208-664-0212
Web: www.cdapress.com

Hagerman Valley Fishwrap
1121 A E. 2900 South
Hagerman, ID 83332
P: 208-837-6304

Idaho County Free Press
P.O. Box 690
Grangeville, ID 83530-0690
P: 208-983-1200

F: 208-983-1336
Web: www.idahocountyfree
press.com

Idaho Falls Post-Register
333 Northgate Mile
Idaho Falls, ID 83401
P: 208-522-1800

Idaho Press-Tribune
P.O. Box 9399
Nampa, ID 83652-9399
P: 208-467-9251
F: 208-467-9562
Web: www.news.mywebpal.com

Idaho Register
303 Federal Way
Boise, ID 83705-5925
P: 208-342-1311
F: 208-342-0224
Web: www.catholicidaho.org

Idaho State Journal
305 S. Arthur
Pocatello, ID 83204
P: 208-232-4161
F: 208-233-8007
Web: www.news.mywebpal.com

Jefferson Star
P.O. Box 37
Rigby, ID 83442-0037
P: 208-745-8701
F: 208-745-8703

Lewiston Morning Tribune
P.O. Box 957
Lewiston, ID 83501-0957
P: 208-743-9411
F: 208-746-7341
Web: www.lmtribune.com

Moscow Pullman Daily News
409 S. Jackson St.
Moscow, ID 83843-2231
P: 208-882-5561
F: 208-883-8205
Web: www.dnews.com

Mountain Home News
P.O. Box 1330
Mountain Home AFB,
ID 83647-1330
P: 208-587-3331
F: 208-587-9205
Web: www.news.mywebpal.com

North Side News
P.O. Box 468
Jerome, ID 83338
P: 208-324-3391

Post Register
333 Northgate Mile
Idaho Falls, ID 83401
P: 208-522-1800
Web: www.idahonews.com

Preston Citizen
75 S. State St.
Preston, ID 83263-1242
P: 208-852-0155
F: 208-852-0158

Salmon Recorder-Herald
519 Van Dreff
Salmon, ID 83467-4228
P: 208-756-2221

Shoshone News-Press
401 Main St.
Kellogg, ID 83837-2600
P: 208-783-1107
F: 208-784-6791

St. Maries Gazette Record
127 S. 7th
St. Maries, ID 83861-1801
P: 208-245-4538
F: 208-245-4991
Web: www.stmariesidaho.com

Star-News
P.O. Box 985
McCall, ID 83638
P: 208-634-2123
Web: www.webdms.com/
~starnews/

Teton Valley News
75 N. Main St.
Driggs, ID 83422
P: 208-354-8101
F: 208-354-8621
Web: www.tetonvalleynews.com

The Crusader
Northwest Nazarene College
Nampa, ID 83651
P: 208-467-8556

The Idaho Statesman
P.O. Box 40
Boise, ID 83707-0040
P: 208-377-6200
P: 800-635-8934
Web: www.idahostatesman.com

The Morning News
P.O. Box 70
Blackfoot, ID 83221-2719
P: 208-785-1100
F: 208-785-4239
Web: www.am-news.com

The News-Examiner
P.O. Box 278
Montpelier, ID 83254
P: 208-847-0552
Web: www.news-examine.net

The South Idaho Press
P.O. Box 190
Burley, ID 83318-0190
P: 208-678-2201
F: 208-678-0412
Web: www.southidahopress.com

The Times-News
P.O. Box 548
Twin Falls, ID 83301-5842
P: 208-733-0931
F: 208-734-5538
Web: www.magicvalley.com

Wood River Journal
11 E. Bullion
Hailey, ID 83333
P: 208-788-3444
F: 208-788-0083
Web: www.wrjournal.com

Montana Book Publishers

Backcountry Publishing
Matt Richards
P.O. Box 343
Rexford MT 59930
P: 406-955-5650

Big Mountain Publishing
220 2nd St. East
Whitfish MT 59937
P: 406-862-7297
F: 406-862-8740

Poetry, non-fiction,
tourist guides.

Big Sky Publications
5805 Helena Dr.
Missoula MT 59803
P: 406-251-5189

Desktop publishing,
graphic design, bindery and
vanity press.

Blaze Books
Morgan Seanan
929 10th Ave.
Helena MT 59601
P: 406-449-2404
E: blazebooks@aol.com

Boone And Crockett Club
250 Station Dr.
Missoula MT 59801

Publishes books on big game
records, outdoor adventure and
wildlife hunting, conservation
and research.

**Champions
Publishing/Ultimate Press**
1627 West Main St. #148
Bozeman MT 59715
P: 406-585-0712

Web: www.ultimatemontana.com

Publishes the Ultimate Montana
Atlas and Travel Encyclopedia.

Clark City Press
109 W. Callender St.
Livingston, MT 59047
P: 402-222-8789

Non-fiction, query first.

Cottonwood Publishing Inc.
120 Greenwood Dr.
Helena MT 59601
Web: www.oldmontana.com

Publisher of western novels and
comics. Reprints Stan Lynde's
novels, his Rick O'Shay, Latigo
and Grass Roots comic strips.

**Falcon Publishing-Globe
Pequot Press**
555 Fuller Ave.
Helena, MT 59601
P: 406-442-6597

Publishes over 100 hard and
softcover books a year in the
form of hiking and nature
guides, Western histroy,
regional cookbooks, Americana.
Accepts nonfictions, biography,
memoires, photos. Guidelines
and catolog available.

Greycliff Publishing Co.
P.O. Box 1273
Helena, MT 59526
P: 406-443-1888
Web: www.greycliff.com

Publishes hard and soft cover
books on fishing. Query
letter, SASE.

**Griggs Printing
And Publishing**
2 5th Ave.
Havre MT 59526
P: 406-265-7431

Holmlund Distributing
1612 Tompy St.
Miles City MT 59301
P: 406-232-6764
F: 406-232-6061
E: holmlund@midrivers.com
Web: www.earlbook.com

Wally Badgett's cartoon series
The Books of Earl; true to life
humor straight from the ranch
life Wally lives and loves.

**Montana Historical
Society Press**
P.O. Box 201201
Helena, MT 59620-1201
P: 406-444-4708

Thoroughly researched, well-
written manuscripts on the
history of Montana and the
region. Less than 400 pages,
12 pt. double spaced.
Query or send two copies
of your manuscript.

**Mountain Press
Publishing Co.**
P.O. Box 2399
Missoula MT 59806
P: 406-728-1900

F: 406-728-1635
Web: www.mountainpress
publish.com

Hard and softcover books in the
following groups: Roadside
Geology, Roadside History,
birdwatching, plant, wildflower,
Will James, horse, Native
American, fishing, earth science
books. Query with outline,
sample chapters, SASE.

**Pictorial Histories
Publishing Co.**
521 W. Bickford
Missoula MT 59801
P: 406-549-8488

No unsolicited ms. Query
w/SASE. Catalog.

Redwing Publishing
P.O. Box 460448
Huson MT 59846
P: 406-626-4438
F: 406-626-4438*51
E: preg42A@prodigy.com
Web: www.bookmasters.com/
marktplc/books/00101.htm

Rondi Enterprises
530 So. Harris
Helena MT 59601
P: 406-443-6488
F: 406-443-6488
E: dogs4@juno.com

Royal Rags Publishing
P.O. Box 594
Emigrant MT 59027
P: 406-333-4296
F: 406-333-4296

Seven Locks Press
208 N. Montana Ave. #205
Helena MT 59601
P: 406-443-7977
E: sevenloxrox@mt.net

Full service book publisher with
on-line catalog

Skyline Publishing Company
P.O. Box 1118
Columbia Falls MT 59912
P: 406-892-0123
F: 406-892-1922

Spirit Talk Press
Postal Drawer V
Browning MT 59417
P: 406-338-2882

Publishes softcover books
pertaining to Canada and the
US. Accepts fiction, poetry,
cartoons, biographies, nonfiction
reviews, memoirs. Query
w/SASE

**Stoneydale Press
Publishing Co.**
523 Main
Stevensville MT 59870
P: 406-777-2729
Web: www.stoneydale.com

Books associated with the
outdoors and the Northern
Rockies Region. Historical
reminisces centered on
incredible places or early day
outfitting, history of the region,
specifically with regard to Lewis
& Clark's adventures.

Summit University Press

Norman N. Millman
P.O. Box 5000
Corwin Springs MT 59030-5000
P: 406-848-9295
F: 406-848-9290
E: rightsandpermissions
@cut.org

Practical spirituality, esoteric literature, person growth, self-development, spirituality and psychology.

Wilderness Adventure Press, Inc.

45 Buckskin Rd.
Belgrade MT 59714
P: 800-925-3339:

Specializes in sports books, world's largest selection of hunting and fishing books. SASE for quidelines.

Wildlife-Wildlands Institute

5200 Upper Miller Creek Rd.
Missoula MT 59803

Animals, conservation and natural history. Write for quidelines.

Wisdom House Publications

Marjorie A. Lombard
P.O. Box 79
Emigrant MT 59027
P: 406-333-4665

Word Wrangler

Barbara Quanbeck
332 Tobin Creek Rd.
Livingston MT 59047
P: 406-686-4230

F: 406-686-4230
E: wrdwranglr@aol.com

An e-Publisher and online Bookstore. We publish and sell all genres, however, we do not accept manuscripts containing disparaging content concerning race, religion, or gender.

Montana Periodicals

Agri-News

P.O. Box 30755
Billings, MT 59107-0755
P: 406-259-4589

Ag Almanac

P.O. Box 2604
Great Falls, MT 59403

Northern Star

P.O. Box 811
Great Falls, MT 59403-0811
P: 406-453-3035

Montana Magazine

P.O. Box 5630
Helena, MT 59604
P: 406-443-5480
Web: www.montana
magazine.com

Photographs and entertaining, informative writing about Montana.

Montana, The Magazine of Western History

P.O. Box 210201
Helena, MT 59620-1201
P: 406-444-4708
F: 406-444-2696

E: rankinmhs@aol.com
Web: www.his.state.mt.us

Montana Living
14 3rd St. E.
Kalispell, MT 59901
P: 406-756-9777
E: info@montanaliving.com
Web: www.montanaliving.com

BikeReport
P.O. Box 8308
Missoula, MT 59807
P: 406-721-1776

Bugle
P.O. Box 8249
Missoula, MT 59807
P: 406-523-4568
Web: www.rmef.org
Rocky Mountain Elk Federation.

Northern Lights
P.O. Box 8084
Missoula, MT 59807-8084
P: 406-721-7415

Rocky Mt. Child
2801 S. Russell, Ste. 7
Missoula, MT 59801
P: 406-327-0725
Web: www.rockymtnchild.com

Horse & Rider
P.O. Box 8
Stevensville, MT 59870

Montana Newspapers

Anaconda Leader
121 Main St.

Anaconda, MT 59711-2251
P: 406-563-5283
F: 406-563-5284
Web: www.mtnewspapers.com

Big Horn County News
240 N. Center Ave.
Hardin, MT 59034
P: 406-665-1008
F: 406-665-1012
Web: www.mtnewspapers.com

Bigfork Eagle
P.O. Box 406
Bigfork, MT 59911
P: 406-837-5131
F: 406-837-1132
Web: www.mtnewspapers.com

Billings Gazette
P.O. Box 36300
Billings, MT 59107-6300
P: 406-657-1200
P: 800-543-2505
Web: www.billingsgazette.com

Bozeman Daily Chronicle
P.O. Box 1190
Bozeman, MT 59771
P: 406-587-4491
F: 406-587-7995
Web: www.news.mywebpal.com

Carbon County News
P.O. Box 970
Red Lodge, MT 59068
P: 406-446-2222
F: 406-446-2225
Web: www.carboncounty
news.com

Cascade Courier
100 First St.
North Cascade, MT 59421
P: 406-468-9231
F: 406-468-3030
Web: www.mtnewspapers.com

Choteau Acantha
P.O. Box 320
Choteau, MT 59422
P: 406-466-2403
F: 406-466-2403
Web: www.choteauacantha.com

Cut Bank Pioneer Press
P.O. Box 847
Cut Bank, MT 59427
P: 406-873-2201
F: 406-873-2443
Web: www.mtnewspapers.com

Dillon Tribune
P.O. Box 911
Dillon, MT 59725
P: 406-683-2331
F: 406-683-2332
Web: www.mtnewspapers.com

Fairfield Sun Times
P.O. Box 578
Fairfield, MT 59436
P: 406-467-2334
F: 406-467-3354
Web: www.mtnewspapers.com

Glacier Reporter
P.O. Box 349
Browning, MT 59417
P: 406-338-2090
F: 406-338-2410
Web: www.mtnewspapers.com

Glasgow Courier
P.O. Box 151
Glasgow, MT 59230-0151
P: 406-228-9301
F: 406-228-2665
Web: www.glasgowcourier.com

Great Falls Tribune
205 River Dr. S.
Great Falls, MT 59403
P: 406-791-1444
F: 406-791-1431
Web: www.greatfallstribune.com

Havre Daily News
119 2nd St.
Havre, MT 59501
P: 406-265-6795
F: 406-265-6798
Web: www.news.mywebpal.com

Helena Indenpendant Record
P.O. Box 4249
Helena, MT 59604
P: 406-447-4000
P: 800-523-2272
F: 406-477-4052
Web: www.helenair.com

Herald News
P.O. Box 639
Wolf Point, MT 59201-0639
P: 406-653-2222
F: 406-653-2221
Web: www.wolfpoint.com/news/
news.htm

Hungry Horse News
P.O. Box 189
Columbia Falls, MT 59912-0189
P: 406-862-2151
Web: www.hungryhorse
news.com

Independent-Observer
P.O. Box 966
Conrad, MT 59425
P: 406-271-5561
F: 406-271-5562
Web: www.mtnewspapers.com

Judith Basin Press
P.O. Box 507
Stanford, MT 59479
P: 406-566-2471
F: 406-566-2471
Web: www.mtnewspapers.com

Laurel Outlook
P.O. Box 278
Laurel, MT 59044
P: 406-628-4412
F: 406-628-8260
Web: www.laureloutlook.com

Lewistown News-Argus
P.O. Box 900
Lewistown, MT 59457-0900
P: 406-538-3401
F: 406-538-3405
Web: www.lewistownnews.com

Liberty County Times
P.O. Box 689
Chester, MT 59522
P: 406-759-5355
F: 406-759-5261
Web: www.highline.town
news.com

Livingston Enterprise
P.O. Box 2000
Livingston, MT 59047
P: 406-222-2000
F: 406-222-8580
Web: www.livingston
enterprise.com

Miles City Star
P.O. Box 1216
Miles City, MT 59301
P: 406-232-0450
F: 406-232-6687
Web: www.milescitystar.com

Mineral Independent
P.O. Box 387
st. regis, MT 59866
P: 406-649-2078
F: 406-649-2078
Web: www.mtnewspapers.com

Missoulian
P.O. Box 8029
Missoula, MT 59807-8029
P: 406-523-5200
P: 800-366-7102
F: 406-523-5221
Web: www.missoulian.com

Montana Kaimin
University of Montana
Missoula, MT 59812

Montana Standard
25 W. Granite St.
Butte, MT 59701
P: 406-496-5510
P: 800-877-1074
F: 406-496-5551
Web: www.mtstandard.com

Plentywood Herald
111 W. 2nd Ave.
Plentywood, MT 59254
P: 406-765-1150

Polson Flathead Courier
P.O. Box 1091
Polson, MT 59860-1091
P: 406-883-4343

Ranger-Review
P.O. Box 61
Glendive, MT 59330-1614
P: 406-365-3303
F: 406-365-5435
Web: www.rangerreview.com

Ravalli Republic
232 Main St.
Hamilton, MT 59840
P: 406-363-3300
F: 406-363-1767
Web: www.ravallinews.com

Sanders County Ledger
P.O. Box 219
Thompson Falls, MT 59873
P: 406-827-3421
F: 406-827-4375
Web: www.scledger.com

Sidney Herald
310 2nd Ave. NE
Sidney, MT 59270-4119
P: 406-482-2403
F: 406-482-7802
Web: www.sidneyherald.com

Silver State Post
P.O. Box 111
Deer Lodge, MT 59722
P: 406-846-2424
F: 406-846-2453
Web: www.powellpost.com

The Big Timber Pioneer
P.O. Box 830
Big Timber, MT 59011
P: 406-932-5298
Web: www.mtnewspapers.com

The Billings Times
2919 Montana Ave.
Billings, MT 59101
P: 406-245-4994
F: 406-245-5115
Web: www.mtnewspapers.com

The Boulder Monitor
P.O. Box 66
Boulder, MT 59632
P: 406-225-3821
F: 406-225-3821
Web: www.mtnewspapers.com

The Daily Interlake
727 E. Idaho
Kalispell, MT 59901
P: 406-758-4447
Web: www.dailyinterlake.com

The Ekalaka Eagle
P.O. Box 66
Ekalaka, MT 59324
P: 406-775-6245
F: 406-775-8749
Web: www.mtnewspapers.com

The Meagher County News
P.O. Box 349
White Sulphur Springs, MT 59645
P: 406-547-3831
F: 406-547-3832
Web: www.meagherconews.com

The Mountaineer
P.O. Box 529
Big Sandy, MT 55920
P: 406-378-2176
F: 406-378-2176
Web: www.mtnewspapers.com

The Philipsburg Mail
P.O. Box 160
Philipsburg, MT 59858
P: 406-859-3223
F: 406-859-3223
Web: www.philipsburgmail.com

The Phillips County News
P.O. Box 850
Malta, MT 59538
P: 406-654-2020
F: 406-654-1410
Web: www.mtnewspapers.com

The River Press
P.O. Box 69
Fort Benton, MT 59442-0069
P: 406-622-3311
F: 406-622-5446
Web: www.mtnewspapers.com

The Roundup Record Tribune & Winnett Times
P.O. Box 350
Roundup, MT 59072
P: 406-323-1105
F: 406-323-1761
Web: www.mtnewspapers.com

The Searchlight
Wold Point c/o Herald-News
Culbertson, MT 59218
P: 406-787-5821

The Shelby Promoter
P.O. Box 610
Shelby, MT 59474
P: 406-434-5171
F: 406-434-5955
Web: www.mtnewspapers.com

The Stillwater County News
P.O. Box 659
Columbus, MT 59019
P: 406-322-5212
F: 406-322-5391
Web: www.mtnewspapers.com

The Terry Tribune
P.O. Box 127
Terry, MT 59349
P: 406-637-5513
F: 406-637-2149
Web: www.mtnewspapers.com

The Times Clarion
P.O. Box 307
Harlowton, MT 59036
P: 406-632-5633
F: 406-632-5644
Web: www.timesclarion.com

The Wibaux Pioneer-Gazette
P.O. Box 218
Wibaux, MT 59353
P: 406-795-2218
F: 406-795-2218
Web: www.mtnewspapers.com

Three Forks Herald
P.O. Box 586
Three Forks, MT 59752
P: 406-285-3414
F: 406-285-3414
Web: www.mtnewspapers.com

Tobacco Valley News
P.O. Box 307
Eureka, MT 59917
P: 406-296-2514
Web:
www.tobaccovalleynews.com

Townsend Star
P.O. Box 1011
Townsend, MT 59644
P: 406-266-3333
F: 406-266-5440
Web: www.townsendstar.com

Western News
P.O. Box 1377
Libby, MT 59923
P: 406-293-4124
F: 406-293-7187
Web:
www.libby.org/westernnews

Whitefish Pilot
P.O. Box 488
Whitefish, MT 59937
P: 406-862-3505
F: 406-862-3636
Web: www.whitefishpilot.com

Oregon Book Publishers

Alcove Publishing Company
2783 N.E. Kimberly Ct.
McMinnville, OR 97128-2363
P: 503-472-4845
E: alcove@viclink.com
Web: www.alcovebiz.com

Small Business
Management Book

Alder Press
Contact: Fred Barrett
P.O. Box 1503
Portland, OR 97207
P: 503-246-7983
E: alder@teleport.com
www: alderpress.com

Amadeus Press
133 S.W. 2nd Ave., Ste. 450
Portland, OR 97204
P: 503-227-2878
E: info@amadeuspress.com
Web: www.amadeuspress.com

Amadeus Press publishes books
pertaining to classical and
traditional music and opera.

Avant Guard Publications
495 Chestnut St., Ste. 18
Ashland, OR 97520-1577
P: 541-552-0175

Beynch Press Publishing Co.
1928 S.E. Ladd Ave.
Portland, OR 97214
Contact: Alice Cornyn Selby
P: 503-232-0433
E: justalyce@usa.net
Web: www.justalyce.com

Barclay Press
110 S Elliott Rd,
Newberg, OR 97132
P: 503 538-9775
E: info@barclaypress.com
www.barclaypress.com/

Publishing focus reflects Quaker (Friends) values with an emphasis on Christian spirituality and contemporary issues that Christians should address.

The Bear Wallow
809 S. 12th Street
La Grande, OR 97850
P: 541-962-7864
E: bearwallow@uwtc.net

Specializing in quality book production of historic nature.

Beautiful America Publishing Company
Contact: Nancy Hankins
P.O. Box 244
2600 Progress Way
Woodburn, OR 97071
P: 503-982-4616
E: bapco@web-ster.com
Web: beautifulamericapub.com

Books and calendars featuring full color nature photography.

Beyond Words
20827 N.W. Cornell Rd., Ste 500
Hillsboro, OR 97124-9808
P: 503-531-8700
E: info@beyondword.com
Web: www.beyondword.com

Coffee Table/Photography, Children's Picture Books, Young Adult Non-Fiction, Gift, Inspiration, Pet/Nature, Parenting, Women's Interest, Health Books Personal Growth/Psychology, Philosopy/Spirituality, Popular Culture, Native American. No e-mail queries.

Bonanza Publishing
P.O. Box 204
Prineville, OR 97754 USA
P: 800-399-3115
E: bonanza@ricksteber.com Web: www.ricksteber.com/contact.htm

Author/publisher reluctant to label himself strictly as a historian, Rick says, "I'm a combination historian, biographer and storyteller. Most of all, I like to tell a good story that gives the reader a sense of time and place."

Butte Publications
P.O. Box 1328
Hillsboro OR 97123
P: 503-648-9791
E: buttepublications.com
Web: www.butte.publications.com

Resources serving the deaf community.

Calyx
P.O. Box B
Corvallis, OR 97339
Telephone: 541 753 9384
E: calyx@proaxis.com
Web: www.proaxis.com/~calyx/

CALYX exists to nurture women's creativity by publishing fine literary and artistic work by women.

Collectors Press Inc.
P.O. Box 230986
Portland, OR 97281
P: 503-684-3030
E: rperry@collectorspress.com
Web: www.collectorspress.com
Nostalgia, Art.

Crispin/Hammer Publishing
5640 Imai Rd
Hood River, OR 97031-7468
P: 541-806-1190
E: crispinpub@gorge.net
Web: himalayandhaba.com
Author/Publisher.

Deep Well Publishing Co.
1371 Peace st S.E., Ste. 12
Salem, OR 97302-2572
P: 503-581-6339
E: jdmartin2@hotmail.com
Author/Publisher.

Dimi Press
3820 Oak Hollow Lane SE
Salem, OR 97302-4774
P: 503-364-7698
E: dickbook@earthlink.net
Publisher/Author/Consultant.

Firelight Publishing, Inc.
226 Division St. SW
Sublimity, OR 97385
P: 503-767-0444
E: editor@firelight
publishing.com
Web: firelightpublishing.com

First Books
3000 Market St NE, Ste. 527
Salem, OR 97301
P: 503-588-2224

First Mom's Club
205 Fern Valley Road
Medford, OR 97501
P: 541-535-7282
E: Dianne@Cpros.com
Author/Publisher.

Frank Amato Publications, Inc.
P.O. Box 82112
Portland, OR 97282
P: 503-653-8108
E: General Information
info@amatobooks.com
Web: www.amatobooks.com

Future Tense Books
P.O. Box 2416
Portland, OR 97242
E: futuretense@q7.com

Grapevine Publications Inc.,
Mailing address:
    P.O. Box 2449
    Corvallis, OR 97339
Street Address:
    626 N.W. 4th Street
    Corvallis, OR 97330.
P: 541-754-0583
Web: www.read-gpi.com/
about/about-c.htm

Grapevine Publications, Inc. publishes clear and simple explanations of finance, math, science and technology products. No techno-jargon or boring manuals.

Graphic Arts Center Publishing Company
3019 N.W. Yeon
Portland, OR 97210
P: 503-226-2402 x234

E: tricia@gacpc.com
Web: www.gacpc.com

Graphic Arts Center Publishing Company publishes books, calendars, and other products in the subject areas of regional, gardening, photo essay, nature, travel, cooking, and children's. The three imprints are Graphic Arts Center Publishing®, Alaska Northwest Books™, and WestWinds Press.

Graphic Press
606 S. 6th St.
Klamath Falls, OR 97601-6200
P: 541-884-4193

Harvest House Books
1075 Arrowsmith
Eugene, OR 97402
P: 503-343-0123

Currently ranked among the top five American publishers of Christian literature, Harvest House publishes more than 160 new books each year and offers a strong backlist of 600 titles. The company's motto, "Books You Can Believe In™" reflects its reputation for providing affordable, trustworthy and practical books meeting peoples' most current needs.

Hawthorne Books
1524 S.E. 36th Ave.
Portland, OR 97214
P: 503-231-1441

E: info@hawthornebooks.
Web: www.hawthornebooks.com

Publish four to six titles each year. Interested in literary novels and narrative non-fiction aimed at a contemporary audience. Does not publish genre fiction such as Romance, Western, Mysteries, Science Fiction, or children's books.

Lerne-Aderman Enterprises
P.O. Box 4733
Portland, OR 97208
Web: www.lerneradermanbooks.
bigstep.com

Author/publisher humorous look at Jewish life

New Moon Publishing Inc.
P.O. Box 90
Corvallis, OR 97339-0090
P: 541-745-7773
E: tom@growingedge.com
Web: www.growingedge.com

Recreation: gardening, horticulture; Nature

New Sage Press, Inc.
P.O. Box 607
Troutdale, OR 97080
P: 503-95-2211
E: info@newsagepess.com
Web: www.newsagepress.com

NewSage Press books cover a myriad of interests and social concerns, including the animal and human bond, environmental issues, nature, women's issues, and more.

Night Shade Books
501 S. Willamette St.
Newberg, OR 97132
P: 503-475-7408
E: night@nightshadebooks.com
Web: www.nightshadebooks.com/contact.htm

Night Shade Books is a small press publishing company with a focus on Horror and Weird Fiction. Looking for the fresh, the odd, the type of book on which we would be proud to put the Night Shade Books logo down the spine.

Pastoral Press
5536 N.E. Hassalo
Portland, OR 97213-3638
P: 503-281-1191
E: liturgy@ocp.org
Web: www.ocp.org

Professional books on religion and theology.

Premiere Editions Int'l
2397 N.W. Kings Blvd., Ste. 311
Corvallis, OR 97330
P: 541-752-4239
E: publish@premier-editions.com
Web: www.premiere editions.com

Biogaphy. Memoirs.

Prescott Street Press
P.O. Box 40312
Portland, Or 97240
P: 503-254-2922

Fiction/Poetry/Literature

Questar Publishers, Inc.
305 West Adams Street
P.O. Box 1720
Sisters, OR 97759
P: 503-549-1144

Simar Enterprises
P.O. Box 1400
Sutherlin, OR 97479
P: 541-459-0927
F: 541-459-5587
E: simarent@yahoo.com
Web: www.galaxymall.com/site/subud
Web: www.Subud.ws

Spirituality

Three Oaks Farm
P.O. Box 1240
Ashland, OR 97520-0055
P: 541- 512-8792
Web: www.storylinepress.com/slpstory.html
E: mail@storylinepress.com

Poetry: Story Line Press books Story Line declared itself a true home for poetry, open to new and seasoned voices alike. Seventeen years and over 200 volumes of serious literature later, Story Line has published Pulitzer Prize winners, discovered important new authors, sustained significant writers in mid-career. Its books and authors have received numerous awards.

Timber Press
133 S.W. 2nd Ave, Ste. 450
Portland, OR 97204

P: 503-227-2878
E: neal@timberpress.com
Web: timberpress.com
Horticulture and botany.

Traprock Books
1330 East 25th Ave.
Eugene, OR 97403
P: 541-344-1053
Poetry.

TripleTree Publishing
P.O. Box 5684
Eugene, OR 97405
Contact: Liz Cratty
P: 541-338-3184
www.TripleTreePub.com
An exclusive publisher of uncommon fiction.

Walking Tree Press
P.O. Box 871
Pleasant Hill, OR 97455
P: 541-744-1773
E: post@walkingtree.com
Walking Tree Press is a small independent publishing company located in the rural Willamette Valley of western Oregon, where trees grow very tall-but never walk. Walking Tree Press publishes books that contribute to our knowledge of the world, books that are beautiful to look at and handle, and books that inspire us to move in new directions.

White Cloud Press
Contact: Steven Scholl
P.O. Box 3400

Ashland, OR 97520
P: 541-488-6415
Web: whitecloudpress.com
General trade, emphasis on religion and memoirs.

WW West Inc
Contact: Don Compton
20875 Sholes Rd
Bend, OR 97702
P: 541-385-8911
E: wwwest@coinet.com
Author/Publisher.

Oregon Periodicals

**1000 Friends of
Oregon Newsletter**
534 S.W. 3rd Ave., Ste. 300
Portland, OR 97204
P: 503-497-1000
F: 503-223-0073
Web: www.friends.org
Issues of oregon land use and development.

**American Indian Basketry
Magazine**
P.O. Box 66124
Portland, OR 97290
P: 503-233-8131
Institute for the study of traditional American Indian Arts.

The Asian Reporter
922 N. Killingsworth St., Ste. 1A
Portland, OR 97217
P: 503-283-4440
F: 503-283-4445
Web: www.asianreporter.com

Audubon Warbler
5151 NW Cornell Rd
Portland, OR 97210
P: 503-292-6855
Web: www.audubonportland.org

A monthly magazine published
for members.

Backwoods Home Magazine
P.O. Box 712
Gold Beach, OR 97444
P: 541-247-8900
F: 541-247-8600
Web: www.backwoodshome.com

Dedicated to a self-sufficient
life style.

**Beaverton Arts
Commission Newsletter**
P.O. Box 4755
Beaverton, OR 97075

Educational Digest

The Bear Deluxe
P.O. Box 10342
Portland, OR 97296
P: 503-242-1047
Web: www.orlo.org

Exploring environmental issues
through the creative arts.

The Bee
1837 S.E. Harold St.
Portland, OR 97202
P: 503-232-2326
F: 503-232-9787
Web: www.readthebee.com

Black Sheep Newsletter
25455 N.W. Dixie Mountain Rd.

Scappoose, OR 97056
P: 503-621-3063
Web: www.members.aol.com/
jkbsnweb

Articles on fiber producing
animals, their husbandry and
the use of their fibers.

The Blood-Letter
P.O. Box 8251
Portland , OR 97207
P: 503-246-0759
Web: www.friendsofmystery.org

Friends of mystery newsletter.

The Bridal Connection
7000 S.W. Hampton, Ste 130
Portland, OR 97223
Web: www.thebridal
connection.com/

Profiles, relationships, self-help
in marriage preparation.

The Business Journal
851 S.W. Sixth Ave., Ste. 500
Portland, OR 97204
P: 503-274-8733
F: 503-227-2650
E: portland@bizjournals.com
Web: www.bizjournals.com/
portland/

Weekly periodical covering
business in the greater
Portland area.

**Calyx, A Journal of Art &
Literature by Women**
P.O. Box B
Corvallis, OR 97339
P: 503-753-9384

F: 503-753-0515

Web: www.proaxis.com/~calyx

Cascade Cattleman

P.O. Box 1390

Klamath Falls, OR 97601

P: 541-885-4460

F: 541-885-4447

Web: www.news.mywebpal.com

Cascades East

716 NE 4th St.

Bend, OR 97701

P: 541-382-0127

F: 541-382-7057

Web: www.sun-pub.com

Recreation and general interest Central Oregon.

Cascade Horseman

P.O. Box 1390

Klamath Falls, OR 97601

P: 541-885-4460

F: 541-885-4447

Web:

www.cascadehorseman.com

Christian Parenting Today

P.O. Box 3850

Sisters, OR 97759

Bimonthly magazine of evangelical Christian parenting of children from birth through teen years.

Computer Bits

P.O. Box 329

Forest Grove, OR 97116-0329

P: 503-359-9107

Web: www.computerbits.com

Crook County Historical Society Newsletter

246 N. Main

Prineville, OR 97754

Irregular periodical.

Cumtux

1618 Exchange St.

Astoria, OR 97103

P: 503-325-2203

Quarterly journal. Clatsop County Historical Society.

Dog Nose News

5519 N.E. 30TH AVE

Portland, OR 97211

P: 503-281-2041

F: 503-281-2309

Web: www.dognosenews.com

Resource guide information source for animal lovers in the Portland area.

Dwelling Portably

P.O. Box 190-MW

Philomath, OR 97370

Newsletter.

Fedora

P.O. Box 577

Siletz, OR 97380

Periodical.

Flyfishing
P.O. Box 82112
Portland, OR 97282
P: 503-653-8108
F: 503-653-2766
Web: www.combinedbook.com

Forest Perspectives
4033 S.W. Canyon Rd.
Portland, OR 97221
P: 503-288-1367

Periodical on forestry & forest
practices.

The Gated Wye
Office of State Fire Marshall
Salem, OR 97305-1760
P: 503-378-4464

Monthly of timely items and
important features for the fire
service.

Glimmer Train Press, Inc.
710 S.W. Madison St., Ste. 504
Portland, OR 97205
P: 503-221-0836
F: 503-221-0837
Web: www.glimmertrain.com

Heritage
35145 Balboa Pl. S.E.
Albany, OR 97321

Home Power Magazine
P.O. Box 520
Ashland, OR 97520-0520
P: 541-512-0201
F: 541-512-2343
Web: www.homepower.com

Journal of home-made power.

Hortus Northwest
P.O. Box 955
Canby, OR 97013
P: 503-266-7968

Annual directory-journal,
commercial sources for PNW
native plants.

Hubbub, A Poetry Magazine
5344 SE 38th Ave.
Portland, OR 97202
P: 503-775-0370

Nationally circulated biannual
magazine of poetry.

In Stride Magazine
12675 S.W. 1st
Portland, OR 97005
Periodical.

The Jewish Review
6800 S.W. capitol hwy ste b
Portland, OR 97219
P: 503-245-4340
F: 503-245-4342
Web: www.jewishreview.org

Justout
P.O. Box 14400
PORTLAND, OR 97291-0400
P: 503-236-1252
F: 503-236-1257
Web: www.justout.com

Gay and lesbian issues.

KSOR Guide to the Arts
1250 Siskiyou Boulevard
Ashland, OR 97520
Periodical.

**Lariat Horsemanís
Newspaper**
12675 S.W. First St.
Beaverton, OR 97005

Monthly devoted to horses and
related subjects.

Luno Newsletteer
31960 Chin St.
Boring, OR 97009
P: 503-663-5153
E: luno@cse.com

New Connexion
P.O. Box 80397
Portland, OR 97280
P: 503-892-2300
Web: www.newconnexion.net

Journal of conscious evolution.

North Morrow Times
P.O. Box 907
Boardman, OR 97818
P: 541-481-9260
F: 541-481-7354

Northwest Labor Press
P.O. Box 13150
Portland, OR 97213
P: 503-288-3311
F: 503-288-3320
Web: www.nwlaborpress.org

News and views about organized
labor in the Pacific Northwest.

Northwest Palate
P.O. Box 10860
Portland, OR 97796-0860
P: 503-224-6039
F: 503-222-5312

Web: www.nwpalate.com

Wine, food and travel in the
Pacific Northwest.

Northwest Senior Life
PMB 331 15033 S.E. Mcloughlin
Blvd.
Portland, OR 97267
P: 503-630-5160

Items of interest to senior
citizens.

Northwest Travel
Florence, OR 97439
P: 541-997-8401
F: 541-997-1124
Web: www.owhy.com

Bi-monthly travel guide.

OMGA Northwest Newsletter
Oregon Master Gardener
Association
Albany, OR 97321

Periodical devoted to home
gardening.

Oregon Business Magazine
610 S.W. Broadway
Portland, OR 97205
P: 503-223-0304
F: 503-221-6544

Oregon Coast Magazine
4969 Hwy 101, Ste. 2
Florence, OR 97439
P: 541-997-8401
F: 541-997-1124
Web: www.owhy.com

Oregon Commentator
P.O. Box 30128
Eugene, OR 97403
P: 541-686-3721
Web: www.oregon
commentator.com
Opinion journal.

Oregon Cycling
455 W First Ave.
Eugene, OR 97401
P: 541-686-9885
F: 541-686-1015
Web: www.efn.org/~ocycling

Oregon Historical Quarterly
1230 S.W. Park Ave.
Portland, OR 97205-2483
Web: www.ohs.org/publications

Oregon Horseman
3525 Garden Ave.
Springfield, OR 97478

Oregon Humanities
812 S.W. Washington St., Ste. 225
Portland, OR 97205
P: 503-241-0543
Web: www.oregonhum.org

Oregon Writers Colony
P.O. Box 1520
Portland, OR 97293-5200
P: 503-827-8072
E: richen@hevanet.com
Web: www.oregonwriters
colony.org

Oregon Hunters Magazine
P.O. Box 1706
Medford, OR 97501
P: 541-772-7313

F: 541-772-0964
Web: www.oregonhunter.org
Magazine of Oregon Hunters
Association.

The Oregon Peaceworker
104 Commercial St. N.E.
Salem, OR 97301
P: 503-585-2767
Web: www.oregonpeace
works.org
Monthly newsletter.

Oregon Snowmobile News
P.O. Box 6328
Bend, OR 97708
Monthly of the Oregon State
Snowmobiling Assoc.

Oregon State Trooper
P.O. Box 717
Tualatin, OR 97062
Magazine published 3 times a yr.

Paddlewheel Press
P.O. Box 230220
Tigard, OR 97223
Quarterly.

Pharmaceutical Executive
P.O. Box 10460
Springfield, OR 97440
Monthly trade journal.

Portland Parent
8196 S.W. Hall Blvd., Ste. 357
Beaverton, OR 97008
P: 503-626-4940
F: 503-626-4830
Web: www.parenthood.com

The Quarterdeck Review
Columbia River Maritime
Museum
Astoria, OR 97103
P: 503-325-2323
Quarterly for museum
members.

Resource Recycling
P.O. Box 42270
Portland, OR 97242-0270
P: 503-233-1305
F: 503-233-1356
Web: www.resource-
recycling.com
Recycling and
composting journal.

The Riggs Institute
Beaverton, OR 97005
P: 503-646-9459
E: riggs@riggsinst.org
Web: www.riggsinst.org/uc.htm
Periodical.

Ruralite
P.O. Box 558
Forest Grove, OR 97116
P: 503-357-2105
F: 503-357-8615
Web: www.home.europa.com/
~ruralite

Salmon Trout Steelheader
Portland, OR 97282
P: 503-653-8108
Salmon and trout fishing
of Northwest.

Screenings
P.O. Box 13293
Portland, OR 97213
Web: www.oregon
archeological.org
Oregon Archeological Society.

Skies America
P.O. Box 4005
Beaverton, OR 97076
P: 503-520-1955
Web: www.nwa.com/services/
onboard/wtraveler/
In-flight magazine.

Skipping Stones
P.O. Box 3939
Eugene, OR 97208-0939
P: 541-342-4956
Web: www.treelink.com/
skipping
Multi-cultural children's
magazine.

Small Farmers Journal
P.O. Box 1627
Sisters, OR 97759-1627
P: 541-549-2064
F: 541-549-4403
Web: www.smallfarmers
journal.com
Periodical on natural farming
and stock raising.

The Southeast Examiner
P.O. Box 14791
Portland, OR 97293-0791
P: 503-254-7550
F: 503-254-7545
Web: www.southeast
examiner.com

Street Roots
1231 S.W. Morrison
Portland, OR 97205
P: 503-228-5657
Web: www.st.roots.org
Advocate for the homeless.

Talking Leaves
81868 Lost Vallely Ln.
Dexter, OR 97431
P: 503-342-2974
Web: www.talkingleaves.org
Ecological culture journal.

Trabuco Publishing
9265 SW Edgewood Street
Tigard, OR 97223-5911
P: 503-620-5741
E: denver_sasser@hotmail.com

Transformation Times
P.O. Box 425
Beavercreek, OR 97004

Umatilla County Historical Society News
P.O. Box 253
Pendleton, OR 97801
Quarterly.

Willamette Law Review
245 Winter St.
Salem, OR 97301
P: 503-375-5436
Web: www.willamette.edu/wucl/lawreview/
Quarterly journal.

The Willamette Writer
9045 S.W. Barber Blvd., Ste. 5A
Portland, OR 97219-4027
P: 503-452-1552
F: 503-452-0372
E: www.willametewriters.com

The Wordsmith Collection
P.O. Box 22
Lake Oswego, OR 97034-0003
P: 503-697-1670
Web: www.wordsmith collection.com
Publication for creative arts and literature.

Writers NW
Media Weavers, L.L.C.
PO Box 86190
Portland, OR 97266-0190
F: 503-771-5166
E: mediaweavers@attbi.com
News and reviews for the community of the printed word in the Northwest.

Yoga Northwest Magazine
747 S.W. Green Ave.
Portland, OR 97205
P: 503-224-1751
Resource for holistic activities in the Pacific Northwest.

Oregon Newspapers

Albany Democratic-Herald
P.O. Box 130
Albany, OR 97321
P: 541-926-2211
F: 541-926-5298
Web: www.dhonline.com

Argus Observer
P.O. Box 130
Ontario, OR 97914
P: 541-889-5387
P: 800-945-4223
F: 541-889-3347
Web: www.argusobserver.com

Bandon Western World
P.O. Box 248
Bandon, OR 97411
P: 541-347-2423
Web:
www.bandonbythesea.com/west
ernworld

**Behind The Scenes Cascade
Blues Association**
Portland, OR 97214-0493
P: 503-223-1850
F: 503-223-1850
Web: www.cascadeblues.org

Blue Mountain Eagle
195 N. Canyon Blvd.
John Day, OR 97845
P: 541-575-0710
F: 541-575-1244
Web: www.bluemountain
eagle.com

Burns Times-Herald
1777 S.W. Chandler Ave.
Burns, OR 97720
P: 541-382-1811
F: 541-383-0372

Canby Herald
P.O. Box 1108
Canby, OR 97013
P: 503-266-6831
Web: www.canbyherald.com

Cannon Beach Gazette
P.O. Box 888
Cannon Beach, OR 97110
P: 503-436-2812
F: 503-436-1562

Web: www.cannonbeach
gazett.com

Capital Press
P.O. Box 2048
Salem, OR 97308
P: 800-882-6789
F: 503-370-4383
Web: www.capitalpress.com

Cascadia Times
25-6 N.W. 23rd Pl., Ste. 406
Portland, OR 97210-3545
P: 503-223-9036
Web: www.cascadia.times.org

Catholic Sentinel
P.O. Box 18030
Portland, OR 97213
P: 503-281-1191
F: 503-460-5496
Web: www.sentinel.org

Central Oregonian
558 N. Main
Prineville, OR 97754
P: 541-447-6205
F: 541-447-1754
Web: www.central
oregonian.com

Clackamas County News
P.O. Box 549
Estacada, OR 97023
P: 503-630-3241

Clatskanie Chief
P.O. Box 8
Clatskanie, OR 97016
P: 503-728-3350
F: 503-728-3350
Web: www.clatskanie.com/chief

Coquille Valley Sentinel
P.O. Box 400
Coquille, OR 97423
P: 541-396-3191

Corvallis Gazette Times
P.O. Box 368
Corvallis, OR 97339
P: 541-753-2641
F: 541-758-9505
Web: www.gtconnect.com

Courier 004
Chemeketa Community College
Salem, OR 97309
P: 503-399-5134

Curry Coastal Pilot
P.O. Box 700
Brookings, OR 97415
P: 541-469-3123
F: 541-469-4679
Web: www.currypilot.com

Curry County Reporter
P.O. Box 766
Gold Beach, OR 97444
P: 541-247-6643
F: 541-247-6644
Web: www.currycounty
reporter.com

Daily Journal of Commerce
P.O. Box 10127
Portland, OR 97210
P: 503-226-1311
F: 503-224-7140
Web: www.djc-or.com

Dayton Tribune
P.O. Box 69

Dayton, OR 97114
P: 503-864-2310
F: 503-864-2310
Web: www.orenews.com

Dead Mountain Echo
P.O. Box 900
Oakridge, OR 97463
P: 541-782-4241
F: 541-782-3323

East Oregonian
P.O. Box 1089
Pendleton, OR 97801
P: 541-276-2211
Web: www.eastoregonian.com

El Hispanic News
P.O. Box 306
Portland, OR 97207-0306
P: 503-228-3139
F: 503-228-3384
Web: www.hispnews.com

Eugene Weekly
1251 Lincoln
Eugene, OR 97401
P: 541-484-0519
F: 541-484-4044
Web: www.eugeneweekly.com

Grants Pass Daily Courier
P.O. Box 1468
Grants Pass, OR 97528-0330
P: 541-474-3700
Web: www.thedailycourier.com

Gresham Outlook
1190 N.E. Division St.
Gresham, OR 97030
P: 503-665-2181

F: 503-665-2187
Web: www.news.mywebpal.com

Headlight Herald
P.O. Box 444
Tillamook, OR 97141
P: 503-842-7535
F: 503-842-8842
Web: www.tillamookheadlight
herald.com

Heppner Gazette-Times
P.O. Box 337
Heppner, OR 97836
P: 541-676-9228
F: 541-676-9211
Web: www.smalltownpapers.com

Herald & News
P.O. Box 788
Klamath Falls, OR 97601-0320
P: 541-883-4410
F: 541-883-4007
Web: www.heraldandnews.com

Hillsboro Argus
P.O. Box 588
Hillsboro, OR 97123
P: 503-684-1131
F: 503-648-9191
Web: www.hillsboroargus.com

Hood River News
Hood River, OR 97031
P: 541-386-1234
Web: www.hoodrivernews.com

Illinois Valley News
P.O. Box 1370
Cave Junction, OR 97523
P: 541-592-2541
F: 541-592-4330

Jefferson Review
145 S. Main St.
Jefferson, OR 97352
P: 541-327-2241
Web: www.thejefferson
review.com

Keizer Times
142 Chemawa Rd. N.
Keizer, OR 97303-5356
P: 503-390-1051
F: 503-390-8023
Web: www.keizertimes.com

Lake County Examiner
739 N. Second St.
Lakeview, OR 97630
P: 541-947-3378
F: 541-947-4359
Web: www.lakecountyexam.com

Lake Oswego Review
P.O. Box 548
Lake Oswego, OR 97034
P: 503-635-8811
F: 503-635-8817
Web: www.lakeoswego
review.com

Lebanon Express
P.O. Box 459
Lebanon, OR 97355-0459
P: 541-258-3151
Web: www.lebanon-express.com

Malheur Enterprise
P.O. Box 310
Vale, OR 97918
P: 541-473-3377
F: 541-473-3268

Molalla Pioneer
P.O. Box 168
Molalla, OR 97038
P: 503-829-2301
F: 503-829-2317
Web: www.molallapioneer.com

Multnomah Village Press
P.O. Box 80351
Portland, OR 97280
P: 503-244-6933

Myrtle Point Herald
P.O. Box 606
Myrtle Point, OR 97458
P: 541-572-2717
F: 541-572-2828

Newberg Graphic
P.O. Box 700
Newberg, OR 97132
P: 503-538-2181
F: 503-538-1632

Newport News-Times
P.O. Box 965
Newport, OR 97365
P: 541-265-8571
F: 541-265-3862
Web: www.newportnews
times.com

News Register
P.O. Box 727
McMinnville, OR 97128
P: 503-472-5114
P: 800-472-1198
F: 503-472-9151
Web: www.newsregisgter.com

News-Times
P.O. Box 408
Forest Grove, OR 97116
P: 503-357-3181
F: 503-359-8456

Northwest Comic News
P.O. Box 11825
Eugene, OR 97440
P: 503-344-1922

Northwest Labor Press
P.O. Box 13150
Portland, OR 97213
P: 503-288-3311
F: 503-288-3320
Web: www.nwlaborpress.org

Ourtown
213 S.W. Ash St. Suite 207
Portland, OR 97204
P: 503-224-1774
F: 503-224-2-80
Web: www.ourtownmag.com

Pendleton Record
P.O. Box 69
Pendleton, OR 97801
P: 541-276-2853
F: 541-278-2916

Pioneer Log
Lewis and Clark College
Portland, OR 97219-7899
P: 503-293-2651
F: 503-768-7146

**Polk County
Itemizer-Observer**
P.O. Box 108
Dallas, OR 97338
P: 503-623-2373
F: 503-623-2395
Web: www.itemizerobserfer.com

Port Orford News
P.O. Box 5
Port Orford, OR 97465
P: 541-332-2361
F: 541-332-8101
Web: www.portorfordnews.com

Portland Family Magazine
P.O. Box 33136
Portland, OR 97292
P: 503-255-3286
F: 503-261-8945

Redmond Spokesman
P.O. Box 788
Redmond, OR 97756
P: 541-548-2184
F: 541-548-3203

Seaside Signal
P.O. Box 848
Seaside, OR 97138
P: 503-738-5561
F: 503-738-5672
Web: www.seasidesignal.com

Senior News
P.O. Box 229
Salem, OR 97308
P: 503-399-8478
F: 503-399-1645

Spilyay Tymoo
P.O. Box 870
Warm Springs, OR 97761
P: 541-475-3710

St. Johns Review
700 N. Hayden Island Dr.
Portland, OR 97217
P: 503-283-5086

Stayton Mail
P.O. Box 400
Stayton, OR 97383
P: 503-769-6338
F: 503-769-6207
Web: www.eastvalleynews.com

Sun Enterprise
258 Monmouth St.
Independence, OR 97351-2424
P: 503-838-3467

Sweet Home News
P.O. Box 39
Sweet Home, OR 97386
P: 541-367-2135
F: 541-367-2137
Web: www.sweethomenews.com

The Baker City Herald
P.O. Box 807
Baker City, OR 97814
P: 541-523-3673
P: 800-318-7508
F: 541-523-6426
Web: www.bakercityherald.com

The Bee
1837 S.E. Harold St.
Portland, OR 97202
P: 503-232-2326
F: 503-232-9787
Web: www.readthebee.com

The Bookmark
Multnomah County Library
Portland, OR 97212-3796
P: 503-248-5469
TDD: 503-248-5246

The Bridge
Portland Community College
Portland, OR 97219-7199
P: 503-244-4181
F: 503-452-4956

The Bulletin
P.O. Box 6020
Bend, OR 97708-6020
P: 541-382-1811
F: 541-385-5802
Web: www.bendbulletin.com

The Chronicle
P.O. Box 1153
St. Helens, OR 97051
P: 503-397-0116
F: 503-397-4093
Web: www.orenews.com

The Chronicle/The Guide
244 W. Oregon Ave.
Creswell, OR 97426
P: 503-895-2197

The Columbia Press
P.O. Box 130
Warrenton, OR 97146
P: 503-861-3331
F: 503-861-3331

The Courier
P.O. Box 268
Reedsport, OR 97467
P: 541-271-3633
F: 541-271-3138

The Crescent
George Fox College
Newberg, OR 97132
P: 503-538-8383

The Daily Astorian
P.O. Box 210
Astoria, OR 97103
P: 503-325-3211
F: 503-325-6573
Web: www.dailyastorian.com

The Daily Tidings
1661 Siskiyou Blvd.
Ashland, OR 97520
P: 541-482-3456
Web: www.dailytidings.com

The Dalles Daily Chronicle
P.O. Box 1910
The Dalles, OR 97058
P: 541-296-2141
F: 541-298-1365
Web: www.thedalles
chronicle.com

The Drain Enterprise
P.O. Box 26
Drain, OR 97435-0026
P: 541-836-2241
F: 541-836-2243
Web: www.354.com/drain/
enterprise.htm

The Hermiston Herald
193 E. Main
Hermiston, OR 97838
P: 541-567-6457
F: 541-567-4125
Web: www.hermistonherald.com

The Hollywood Star
2000 N.E. 42nd St.
Portland, OR 97213
P: 503-282-9392

F: 503-282-9628
Web:
www.hollywoodstarnews.info

The Madras Pioneer
241 S.E. 6TH
Madras, OR 97741
P: 541-475-2275
F: 541-475-3710
Web: www.madraspioneer.com

The Mail Tribune
P.O. Box 1108
Medford, OR 97501
P: 541-776-4455
F: 541-776-4376
Web: www.mailtribune.com

The Mill City Enterprise
117 N.E. Wall
Mill City, OR 97360
P: 503-897-2772

The New Era Newspaper
1200 Long St.
Sweet Home, OR 97386
P: 503-367-2135

The News Guard
P.O. Box 848
Lincoln City, OR 97367
P: 541-994-2178
F: 541-994-7613
Web: www.thenewsguard.com

The News-Review
P.O. Box 1248
Roseburg, OR 97470
P: 541-672-3321
F: 541-957-4270
Web: www.newsreview.info

The Observer
P.O. Box 3170
La Grande, OR 97850
P: 541-963-3161
Web: www.lagrande
observer.com

The Oregonian
1320 S.W. Broadway
Portland, OR 97201
P: 503-221-8279
F: 503-294-4199
Web: www.oregonian.com

The Register-Guard
P.O. Box 10188
Eugene, OR 97440-2188
P: 541-485-1234
Web: www.registerguard.com

The Sandy Post
P.O. Box 68
Sandy, OR 97055
P: 503-668-5548
F: 503-665-2187
Web: www.orenews.com

The Silverton Appeal-Tribune
P.O. Box 35
Silverton, OR 97381
P: 503-873-8385
Web: www.eastvallelynews.com/
appeal

The Siuslaw News
P.O. Box 10
Florence, OR 97439
P: 541-997-3441
F: 541-997-7979
Web: www.orenews.com

The Skanner
2337 N. Williams
Portland, OR 97228
P: 503-287-3562
F: 503-284-8200

The South County Spotlight
P.O. Box C
Scappose, OR 97056
P: 503-543-6387
F: 503-543-6380
Web: www.columbia
center.org/newsspot

The Southeast Examiner
P.O. Box 14791
Portland, OR 97293
P: 503-234-1770
F: 503-234-1770

The Springfield News
1887 Laura St.
Springfield, OR 97477
P: 503-746-1671
Web: www.springfieldnews.com

The Statesman Journal
P.O. Box 13009
Salem, OR 97309
P: 503-399-399-6773
Web: www.statesman
journal.com

The Sun
P.O. Box 68
Sheridan, OR 97378
P: 503-843-2312
F: 503-843-3830
Web: www.sheridansun.com

The Sun Tribune
104 E. Central
Sutherlin, OR 97479
P: 503-459-2261

The Times
P.O. Box 278
BrownSville, OR 97327
P: 541-466-5311
F: 541-466-5312

The Times-Journal
P.O. Box 746
Condon, OR 97823
P: 541-384-2421
F: 541-384-24111

The World
P.O. Box 1840
Coos Bay, OR 97420
P: 541-269-1222
F: 541-267-0294
Web: www.theworldlink.com

Tillamook Headlight-Herald
1908 2nd St.
Tillamook, OR 97141
P: 503-842-7535

Umpqua Free Press
P.O. Box 729
Myrtle Creek, OR 97457
P: 541-863-5233
F: 541-863-5233

Wallowa County Chieftan
P.O. Box 338
Enterprise, OR 97828
P: 541-426-4567
F: 541-426-3921
Web:
www.wallowa.com/chieftain

West Lane News
P.O. Box 188
Veneta, OR 97487
P: 541-935-1882
F: 541-935-4082

Western RV News
64470 Sylvan Loop
Bend, OR 97701
P: 541-318-8089
F: 541-318-0849
Web: www.westernrvnews.com

Willamette Week
822 S.W. 10th Ave.
Portland, OR 97205
P: 503-243-2122
F: 503-243-1115
Web: www.wweek.com

Woodburn Independent
P.O. Box 96
Woodburn, OR 97071
P: 503-981-3441
F: 503-981-1235
Web: www.woodburn
independent.com

Writer's NW
P.O. Box 86190
Portland, OR 97286-0190
P: 503-771-0428
F: 503-771-5166

Washington
Book Publishers

74th Street Productions
350 N. 74th Street
Seattle, WA 98103
P: 206-781-1447
E: info@74thstreet.com
Web: www.74thstreet.com

Publishes books for children
and young adults retelling
Shakespeare's plays in story
form; books related to the
performing and literary art;
writers' performance skills.

Arthur H. Clark Company
P.O. Box 14707
Spokane, Wa 99214-0707
P: (Toll-Free): 800-842-9286,
E: clarkbks@mindspring.com

**Alaska Northwest
Publishing Company**
see Graphic Arts Center, page170

Ancient River Publishing
P.O. Box 1329
Duvall, WA 98019
P: 425-788-6193
E: ancientriver@ancientriver.com

Black Heron Press
P.O. Box 95676
Seattle, Wa 98145

Prints 4-6 books a year, primarily
literary fiction. Books only, no
individual stories. Send a one-
page cover letter, including your
manuscript word count query
and SASE.

Blue Begonia Press
Bodylogic, LLC
227 Bellevue Way NE
Bellevue, Wa 98004
P: 425-452-9223
E: bodylogic_books@
Yahoo.com

Brook Bay Books
8 Brook Bay
Mercer Island, WA 98040
P: 206-236-2800
E: mvandervelde@excite.com
Non-fiction books, self-help,
how-to, biography

Bryce Publications
4220 34th Avenue West
Seattle, WA 98199
P: 206-352-5934
E: brycepubs@aol.com
Publishes the I-5 Travel guide.

Bytewrite L.L.C.
P.O. Box 2635
Bellingham, WA 98227
P: 360-671-4428
E: fred@bytewrite.com
Author/Publisher of *An
American Sin.*

Clark (Arthur H.)Co.
P.O. Box 14707
Spokane, WA 99214
P: 509-928-9540
History, regional.

Copper Canyon Press
P.O. Box 271, Building 313
Fort Worden State Park
Port Townsend, WA 98368
P: 360-385-4925
E: contact@copper
canyonpres.org
Copper Canyon Press seeks to
build the awareness of,
appreciation of, and audience for
a wide range of emerging and
established American poets, as
well as poetry in translation from
many of the world's cultures,
classical and contemporary.
The Press publishes poetry
exclusively and has established
an international reputation for
its commitment to its authors,
editorial acumen, and dedication
to expanding the audience
of poetry.

Conch Shell Press
P.O. Box 18967
Seattle, WA 98118
P: 206-290-5624
E: j.thompsondodd@
worldnet.att.net

**Communication Project
Specialists**
P.O. Box 111898
Tacoma, WA 98411
E: Pharrin107@Aol.com
www.patriciaharrington.com

Country Messenger Press
78d Cameron Lake Loop Rd
Okanogan, Wa 98840
P: 509-422-1441
E: siniff@ncidata.com
Edna Siniff, Author/Publisher

Publish short books, usually by
senior citizens, on history and
memories; also poetry and
education book.

Crisp Publications
1525 4th Avenue, Suite 400
Seattle, WA 98101
P: 206-340-1833x3006

Demand Publications
2608 Second Avenue Pmb2450
Seattle, WA 98121
P: 206-935-1750
E: tpoppa9114@cs.com
Web: www.publisher@
druglord.com
Author/Publisher

Denali Group Inc.
2815 NW Pine Cone Dr
Issaquah, WA 980027

**Direct Book Service/Dogwise
Publishing**
701 B Poplar St.
Wenatchee, WA 98801
P: 509-663-9115
E: nathan@dogwise.com

Dog Hollow Press
P.O. Box 22287
Seattle, Wa 98122
Contact; Jan Maher
P: 206-568-1195
E: info@doghollow.com

Eaglemont - PMB 741
15600 NE 8th #B-1
Bellevue, WA 98008
P: 425-462-6618
E: info@eaglemontpress

Eaglemont Press is an
independent publisher of
photographic books exploring
the visual beauty of nature.

**Earthstewards Network
Publications**
P.O. Box 10697
Bainbridge Island, WA 98110
P: 800-561-2909
E: healinpgs@aol.com
Publishing branch of the
nonprofit organization.

Earthtones Press
P.O. Box 411
Vashon Island, WA 98070
P: 206-463-2796
E: kristinaturner@earthlink.net
Cookbooks and Health

Envision Publishing
1426 Harvard Ave. #36
Seattle, WA 98122
P: 206-306-3992
E: lindareed@msn.com

Epicenter Press Inc.
P.O. Box 82368
Kenmore, WA 98028
P: 425-485-6822
E: gksturgis@earthlink.net
Web: www.epicenterpress.com
No telephone inquiries, please.
Does not publish fiction, poetry,
or children's titles. Multiple
submissions are discouraged.
See website for proposal
instructions.

Evergreen Pacific Publishing
18002 15th Ave NE Suite B
Shoreline, WA 98155
Web: evergreenpress.com

Publishes Pacific NW nautical
guides and logbooks.

Fox Mountain Publishing
P.O. Box 1516
Tonasket, WA 98855
P: 509-486-4919
E: info@foxmtnpublishing.com

On-The-Farm Newsletter And
Farm Books Chock Full Of
Ideas, Hints And Tips To Save
Small-Farmers Time And
Money In Their Farming
Adventures. Author/Publisher.

Goodfellow Press Inc.
8522 10th Ave NW
Seattle, WA 98117
P: 206-782-2799
F: 206-706-6352
E: info@goodfellowpress.com
Web: www.goodfellowpress.com

Fiction

Hara Publishing Grp
P.O. Box 19732
Seattle, WA 98011
Attn: Sharyn Hara
P: 425-775-7868
E: harapub@foxinternet.net

Harbor Press
P.O. Box 1656
Gig Harbor, WA 98335
E: hlynn@haraborpress.com

Trade Books On Health,
Psychology And Self
Improvement.

Heron Lake Press
4835 S. Lakeside Dr.
Langley, WA 98260
P: 360-321-4733
E: petra@mixed-emotions.com
Web: www.mixed-emotions.com

Author/Publisher.

Hide & Seek Press
P.O. Box 84403
Seattle, WAa 98124
P: 206-933-2069
E: karen_robbins@msn.com
Web: www.hideandseek
press.com

Magic Books With Interactive
Technology.

Homestead Book Company
P.O. Box 17444
Seattle, WA 98107
P: 206-782-4532
Toll free 1-800-426-6777
E: davet@homesteadbook.com

Recent books published include
The Poor Man's Guide to Seattle
Restaurants, Eastside Eats, The
Good Beer Guide, and most
recently, Seattle Laughs.

ICD Press
6216 23rd Ave. Ne
Seattle, WA 98115
P: 206-526-8562
E: cj@creativesystems.org

ICD Press publishes books and
pamphlets from the institute for

creative development. These focus on creative systems theory and specific topics relating to a healthy future.

Illumination Arts Publishing Co., Inc.

P.O. Box 1865
Bellevue, WA 98009
P: 425-644-7185
E: liteinfo@illumin.com
Web: www.illumin.com/

Illumination Arts publishes high quality, enlightening children's picture books with enduring, inspirational and spiritual values. Our aim is to touch people's lives, with illumination and transformation

Impassio Press

P.O. Box 31905
Seattle, WA 98103
P: 206-632-7675
F: 209-797-7127
E: books@impassio.com
Web: www.impassio.com

Impassio Press publishes only 2-3 titles per year of books up to 300 pages in length. Explore website to become more familiar with our mission and titles.
No disk, fax, or E: submissions.

Japphire, Inc.

6947 Coal Creek Parkway SE, #1000
Newcastle, WA 98059
P: 425-430-0007
E: amy@japphire.com
Web: www.japphire.com

Lighthouse Publishing Group, Inc.

14675 Interurban Ave. S.
Seattle, WA 98168
P: 800-872-7411
Web: www.lighthousebooks.com

Lion's Paw Press

4039 NE 57th St
Seattle, WA 98105
Contact; Stephen Vandergrift
E: info@lionspawpress.com
Web: www.lionspawpress.com

Young adult fiction
Author/Publisher

Lone Pine Publishing

1901 Raymond aVe SW, Suite C
Renton, WA 98055
P: 425-204-5965
E: helenll@mindspring.com

Publishes outdoor, nature, gardening and popular history.

Martingale & Co. Inc.

20205 144th Ave NE
Woodinville, WA 98072
P: 425-483-3313
E: jhamada@martingale-pub.com

How-to-quilt books.

Mountain Garden Publishing, Inc.

P.O. Box 98
Snoqualmie, WA 98065
P: 206-888-0773

Garden Books

The Mountaineers Books
1001 SW Klickitat Way, Suite 201
Seattle, WA 98134
P: 800-553-4453
E: webmail@mountaineers.org
Web: mountaineersbooks.org

Outdoor guidebooks, how-tos,
and adventure narratives

Pickle Point Publishing
P.O. Box 4107
Bellevue, WA 98009
P: 425-641-7424

Pine Orchard
2607 Southeast Blvd B150
Spokane, Wa 99223
P: 509-534-9401
E: pineorch@pineorchard.com
Web: www.pineorchard.com/

Portland Press Inc.
P.O. Box 45010
Seattle, WA 98145
P: 253- 274-8883
Web: www.portlandpress.net/
info.html

In 1992, Portland Press was
established as a small publishing
company dedicated to the
production of books about
glassmaking., Portland Press
produces books, videos, note
cards, postcards and posters in
addition to an exclusive line of
signed studio edition glass and
limited-edition fine prints.

PublishingOnline.com
1200 S. 192nd St., Suite 300
Seattle, WA 98148

P: 206-439-9257
F: 206-246-8154
Web: www.publishingonline.com

Raconteurs Press LLC
1426 Harvard Ave #443
Seattle, WA 98122
P: 206-329-4688
E: tom@raconteurs.com
Web: www.raconteurs.com

Raconteurs Press is a small
press publisher based in Seattle.
Focuses on non-fiction books
including books on wine.

Rose Alley Press
4203 Brooklyn Ave. NE #103a
Seattle, WA 98105-5911
P: 206-633-2725
E: rosealleypress@juno.com

Primarily to publish formal
poetry, cultural commentary,
and pamphlets about writing and
publication.

SCW Publications
1011 Boren #155
Seattle, WA 98101
P: 206-682-1268
E: info@poetswest.com

Poetry, Biography, Histories.

Simon And Barklee, Inc.
2280 E. Whidbey Shores Rd.
Langley, WA 98260
P: 360-730-2360
E: Cwsch@Whidbey.com
Web: www.simonand
barklee.com

Educational Materials.

Stringtown Press
2309 W. 12th Avenue
Spokane, WA 99224
P: 509-624-1497
E: stringwon@earthlink.com

Thistle Press
P.O. Box 732
Bellevue, WA 98009
P: 425-885-3173
E: DuseM@aol.com

Thistle Press publishes guidebooks and non-fiction about the Seattle/Puget Sound area including the Pocket Guide to Seattle.

Thomas-Kalland Publishers
903 E. 38th Avenue
Spokane, WA 99203
P: 590-456-6858
E: sabre5@earthlink.net

Sasquatch Books
615 2nd Avenue
Seattle, WA 98104
Phone; 206-467-4300
Web: www.sasquatchbooks.com

Publisher of books for and from the Pacific Northwest, Alaska, and California — is the nation's premier regional press. Sasquatch Books is considers queries and proposals from authors and agents for new projects that fit into the west coast regional publishing program. Include return postage if you want your materials back. Sasquatch does not recommend e-mailed submissions or queries.

The Stranger
1535 11th Ave. 3rd Floor
Seattle, WA 98122

Timeless Books
P.O. Box 3543
Spokane, Wa 99220-4643
P: 509-838-6652
E: info@timeless.org
Web: www.Timeless.Org

Publishes Works of Swami Sivananda.

Timebridges Publishers LLC
1001 Cooper Point Road SW,
Ste. 140-#176
Olympia, WA 98502
E: info@timebridges
publishers.com

Publishers of fine historical fiction including the novel, India Treasures.

Whispering Pine Press, Inc
P.O. Box 142059
Spokane, WA 99214-2059
P: 509- 927-0404
Web: www.Whisperingpine
press.com

An international publishing house dedicated to providing children, parents, and families with beginning readers, fiction, non-fiction, inspirational, and poetic reading materials that are wholesome, informative, educational, and available in a variety of languages.

Tsuanmi Inc
P.O. Box 100
Walla Walla, WA 99362-0033
E: tsunami@innw.net
Web: www.tsunami-inc.net

"Our new mission is to publish and promote the best of the younger generation of poets along with the best of the mature poets writing in English to create connectivity among the generations. The editor wants your best work, signature poems exhibiting artistic control, intellectual rigor and passionate feeling. Will not consider fiction, haiku, rimed verse or cutsy-wutsy word play." Snail mail submissions are preferred.

Turtle Press
P.O. Box 241
Norland, WA 98358
P: 360-385-3626
F: 360-379-9162
E: trtlbluf@olympus.net

Fiction/Literature.

Washington Periodicals

Alaska Airlines Magazine
2701 1st Ave. #250
Seattle, WA 98121
P: 206-441-5871

ALKI: The Washington Library Association Journal
2702 Hoyt Ave
Everett, WA 98201
P: 425-257-7640
F: 425-257-8016
Web: www.wla.org/alki

Animal People News
P.O. Box 960
Clinton, WA 98236
Web: www.animalpeople
news.org

Astro Mind
P.O. Box 5072
Redondo, WA 98054
P: 206-946-6169

Auto and Flat Glass Journal
P.O. Box 12099
Seattle, WA 98102-0099
P: 206-322-5120

Monthly trade magazine for the auto glass industry.

Bellowing Ark
P.O. Box 55564
Shoreline, WA 98155
P: 206-440-0791

Literary Journal: poetry, fiction, essays.

Business Pulse
1732 Iowa St
Bellingham, WA 98229
P: 360-671-3933
E: ckey@businesspulse.com
Web: www.businesspulse.com

Canoe and Kayak Magazine
P.O. Box 3146
Kirkland, WA 98083
Web: www.canoekayak.
about.com

Claims Magazine
Insurance West
1001 4th Ave Plaza , Ste. 3029

Seattle, WA 98154
P: 800-544-0622
Web: www.claimsmag.com
Insurance Claims, Industry
Issues.

**Columbia The Magazine Of
Northwest History**
WSHS Research Center
315 N Stadium Way
Tacoma, WA 98403
P: 253-798-5918
F: 253-597-4186
E: cdubois@wshs.wa.gov
Web: www.wshs.org/columbia

Continuity Publishing Inc
1300 N. State St. Ste. 105
Bellingham, WA 98225
P: 360-676-0789
Magazine for Retailers of New
age Books, Music and
Merchandise.

Crafts Report
87 Wall Street
Seattle, WA 98121
P: 206-441-3102

Earshot Jazz
3429 Fremont Pl. #308
Seattle, WA 98103
P: 206-547-6763

Earthcare Northwest
8028 35th Ave. N.E.
Seattle, WA 98115-4815
P: 206-523-4483
Web: www.seattleaudubon.org

Exhibition Magazine
221 Winslow Way West
Bainbridge Island, WA 98110
P: 206-842-7901
Web: www.artshum.org

Fishing And Hunting News
Box C-19000
Seattle, WA 98109
P: 206-624-3845

**General Aviation
News & Flyer**
P.O. Box 98786
Tacoma, WA 98498-0786
P: 206-588-1743

Home Education Magazine
P.O. Box 1083
Tonasket, WA 98855-1083
P: 800-486-1351
F: 509-486-2753
E: HEM-info@home-ed-
magazine.com
Web: www.home-ed-
magazine.com
Articles on home education/
learning.

Inland Register
P.O. Box 48
Spokane, WA 99210-0048
P: 509-456-7140

Innkeeping World
P.O. Box 84108
Seattle, WA 98124

International Examiner
622 S. Washington St.
Seattle, WA 98104-2704
P: 206-624-3925
F: 206-624-3046
Web: www.international
examiner.com
Semi-monthly newsletter for
Asian American communities of
Seattle/King County.

Listening Post
P.O. Box 9595
Seattle, WA 98195
P: 206-543-9595

**Manufactured Homes
Magazine**
P.O. Box 55998
Seattle, WA 98155
P: 206-743-0497

Marine Digest
1710 South Norman Street
Seattle, WA 98144
P: 206-709-1840
E: phurme@marinedigest.com
Web: www.marinedigest.com

Massage Magazine
1639 W. 1st Ave.
Spokane, WA 99204
P: 509-326-3955
Web: www.massagemag.com

Mavin
600 1st Ave., Ste. 600
Seattle, WA 98104
P: 206-622-7101
Web: www.mavin.net

Muse of Fire
21 Kruse Rd
Port Angeles, WA 98362-8900
Monthly poetry journal.

New Times
P.O. Box 51186
Seattle, WA 98115

No Depression
P.O. Box 31332
Seattle, WA 98103
P: 206-706-7342
Bi-monthly magazine covering
alternative-country music.

Northwest Boat Travel
P.O. Box 220
Anacortes, WA 98221
P: 509-884-1239
F: 509-884-1239
Web: www.boattravel.com

Northwest Cyclist Magazine
P.O. Box 9272
Seattle, WA 98109
P: 206-286-8566

Northwest Fishing Holes
14505 NE 91st
Redmond, WA 98052-6585

**Northwest Skier &
Northwest Sports**
P.O. Box 95229
Seattle, WA 98145
Monthly magazine.

Oregon Farmer-Stockman
P.O. Box 2160
Spokane, WA 99210-2160

Outdoor Empire Publishing, Inc.
511 Eastlake Ave. E.
Seattle, WA 98109
P: 206-624-3845

Pacific Fishing
1515 N.W. 51st
Seattle, WA 98107
P: 206-789-5333

Puget Sound Business Journal
720 3rd Ave., #800
Seattle, WA 98104-1811
P: 206-583-0701
F: 206-447-8510
E: seattle@bizjournals.com
Web: www.bizjournals.com

Puget Sound Parent
P.O. Box 6932
Tacoma, WA 98407-0932

Racing Wheels
P.O. Box
Vancouver, WA 98668
P: 360-892-5590
F: 360-892-8021
Web: www.racingwheels.net

Radiance Herbs & Massage
113 E. Fifth
Olympia, WA 98501
P: 360-357-5250
Web: www.radianceherbs.com

Salmon Bay Communications
1515 NW 51st St.
Seattle, WA 98107-4735

Saxifrage
312 First Ave N. 2nd Floor
Seattle, WA 98109
P: 206-684-7171
E: saxifrage@plu.edu
Web: www.plu.edu/~saxifrag

Seattle Arts Commission.

Sea Kayaker
P.O. Box 17029
Seattle, WA 98107-0729
P: 206-789-1326
F: 206-781-1141
E: mail@seakayakermag.com
Web: www.seakayakermag.com

Publishes narratives on sea kayaking.

Seafood Leader
1115 N.W. 45th St.
Seattle, WA 98107
P: 206-789-6506
F: 206-789-9193

Trade journal of the seafood industry.

Seattle Bride Magazine
423 Third Ave. West
Seattle, WA 98119

Seattle Gay News
1605 12th Ave., #31
Seattle, WA 98122-2467
P: 206-324-4297
F: 206-322-7188
E: sgn2@sgn.org
Web: www.sgn.org/sgn

Seattle Homes and Lifestyles
1221 East Pike St Ste 204
Seattle, WA 98122
P: 206-322-6699
F: 206-322-2799
Web: www.seattlehomes
mag.com

Seattle Magazine
701 Dexter Ave. N. #101
Seattle, WA 98109-4339
P: 206-284-1750
E: seattle@tigeroak.com
Web: www.seattlemag.com

Senior News
112. 4th Ave. E
Olympia, WA 98501
P: 360-586-3590

Senior Scene
223 N. Yakima
Tacoma, WA 98403-2230
P: 253-272-2278
E: seniormedia@seanet.com
Query with SASE.

Small Towns Institute
P.O. Box 517
Ellensburg, WA 98926-0517

Sports, Etc Magazine
11715 Greenwood Ave North
Seattle, WA 98133
P: 206-418-0747
F: 206-418-0746
E: staff@sportsetc.com
Web: www.sportsetc.com

Stocks & Commodities Magazine
4757 California St. SW
Seattle, WA 98116-4499
P: 206-938-0570
Web: www.traders.com
Magazine for investors and traders who use technical analysis.

Tacoma Arts Commission Newsletter
747 Market St. Room 1036
Tacoma, WA 98402
P: 253-591-5046

Tacoma Reporter
1517 S. Fawcett, Ste 250
Tacoma, WA 98402
P: 253-593-3931
Web: www.aan.org
Alternative weekly.

Tacoma Weekly
P.O. Box 7185
Tacoma, WA 98407
P: 253-759-5773
E: tacomaweekly@
mailexcite.com

The Fishermen's News
4005 20th Ave. W., Ste. 110
Seattle, WA 98199-1291
P: 206-282-7545

The Hispanic News
2318 Second Ave.
Seattle, WA 98121
P: 206-768-0421

The Seattle Press

4128 Fremont N.
Seattle, WA 98103
P: 206-547-9660
E: seattlepress@
seattlepress.com
Web: www.seattlepress.com

The Senior Messenger

202 Mill Plane Blvd.
Vancouver, WA 98660
P: 360-696-8077
F: 306-696-8942
E: st.messenger@
ci.vancouver.wa.us
Web: www.ci.vancouver.wa.us

Articles and stories of interest
to seniors.

The Stranger

1535 11th Ave, 3rd Floor
Seattle, WA 98122
P: 206-323-7101
E: postmaster@thestranger.com
Web: www.thestranger.com

Washington Farmer-stockman

3240 Eastlake Avenue E, Ste. 100
Seattle, WA 98102
P: 206-568-2850
E: www.ruralpress.com

Washington Trails Magazine

1305 4th Ave. #512
Seattle, WA 98101
P: 206-625-1367
Web: www.wta.org

Northwest backcountry
hiking issues.

Western Farmer-Stockman Magazines

P.O. Box 2160
Spokane, WA 99210-1615
P: 509-459-5377

Western Mills Today

P.O. Box 610
Edmonds, WA 98020
P: 206-778-3388

Wheat Life

109 East First
Ritzville, WA 99169-2394
P: 509-659-0610
E: WHeat@wawg.org
Web: www.wawg.org

Young Voices

P.O. Box 2321
Olympia, WA 98507
P: 360-357-4683
F: 360-705-9669
Web: www.youngvoices
magazine.com

Stories, artwork and poems by
elementry, middle, and high
school students.

Washington Newspapers

Aberdeen Daily World

P.O. Box 269
Aberdeen, WA 98520
P: 360-532-4000
Web: www.thedailyworld.com

Advocate

P.O. Box 327
Sprague, WA 99032
P: 509-257-2311

Anacortes American
P.O. Box 39
Anacortes, WA 98221
P: 360-293-3122
F: 360-293-5000
Web: www.goanacortes.com

Bainbridge Review
P.O. Box 10817
Bainbridge Island, WA 98110
Web: www.bainbridge
review.com

Ballard News-Tribune
2208 N.W. Market
Seattle, WA 98017
P: 206-783-1244
Web: www.robinsonnews.com

Bellingham Herald
1155 N. State St.
Bellingham, WA 98225
P: 360-676-2600
F: 360-676-7113
Web: www.bellingham
herald.com

Brewster Quad-City Herald
P.O. Box 37
Brewster, WA 98812
P: 509-689-2507
F: 509-689-2508
Web: www.smalltownpapers.com

**Camas-Washougal
Post-Record**
P.O. Box 1013
Camas, WA 98607
P: 360-834-2141
F: 360-834-3423

Web: www.camaspost
record.com

Cashmere Valley Record
P.O. Box N.
Cashmere, WA 98815
P: 509-782-3781
Web: www.leavenworth
echo.com

**Central Kitsap Reporter/
Washington Newspaper
Pub. Assoc.**
3838 Stone Way N.
Seattle, WA 98102
P: 206-634-3838
F: 206-634-3842
Web: www.wnpa.com

Channel Town Press
P.O. Box 575
LaConner, WA 98257
P: 360-466-3315

Chinook Observer
P.O. Box 427
Long Beach, WA 98631
P: 360-642-8181
Web: www.chinookobserver.com

Columbia Basin Herald
P.O. Box 910
Moses Lake, WA 98837
P: 509-765-4561
Web: www.columbiabasin
herald.com

Cowlitz County Advocate
P.O. Box 368
Castle Rock, WA 98611
P: 360-274-6663

Crosswind
P.O. Box 10
Oak Harbor, WA 98277
P: 360-675-6611

Daily Bulletin
P.O. Box 770
Colfax, WA 99111
P: 509-397-4333

Daily Journal American
1705 - 132nd N.E.
Bellevue, WA 98005
P: 206-455-2222
F: 206-453-4273

Daily Sun News
P.O. Box 878
Sunnyside, WA 98944
P: 509-837-4500
F: 509-837-6397
Web: www.sunnyside.net

Davenport Times
P.O. Box 66
Davenport, WA 99122
P: 509-725-0101
Web: www.wnpa.com

Dayton Chronicle
P.O. Box 6
Dayton, WA 99328
P: 509-382-2221

East Washingtonian
742 Main
Pomeroy, WA 99347
P: 509-843-1313
Web: www.wnpa.com

Edmonds Enterprise
P.O. Box 977

Lynnwood, WA 98046
P: 425-673-6500

Ellensburg Daily Record
401 N. Main St.
Ellensburg, WA 98926-3107
P: 509-925-1414
F: 509-925-5696
Web: www.news.mywebpal.com

Ex Press
P.O. Box 47322
Olympia, WA 98504-7322
P: 360-705-7077
F: 360-705-6806
Web:
www.geubanks@wsdot.wa.gov

Federal Way News
1634 S. 312th
Federal Way, WA 98003
P: 206-932-0300
F: 206-838-7443
Web: www.robinsonnews.com

Forks Forum
494 Forks Ave.
Forks, WA 98331
P: 360-374-3311
Web: www.wnpa.com

Franklin County Graphic
P.O. Box 160
Connell, WA 99326
P: 509-234-3181

Gazette
P.O. Box 770
Colfax, WA 99111
P: 509-397-4333

Gazette-Tribune
P.O. Box 250
Oroville, WA 98844
P: 509-476-3602

Goldendale Sentinel
117 W. Main St.
Goldendale, WA 98620
P: 509-773-3777
P: 888-287-3777
Web: www.gorgenews.com

Grant County Journal
29 Alder SW
Ephrata, WA 98823
P: 509-754-4636
Web: www.wnpa.com

Highline Times & Des Moines News
P.O. Box 518
Burien, WA 98166
P: 206-242-0100

Independent
P.O. Box 27
Port Orchard, WA 98366
P: 360-876-4414
Web: www.portorchard
independent.com

Island Independent
P.O. Box 853
Langley, WA 98260
P: 360-221-8242

Jewish Transcript
Seattle, WA
P: 206-441-4553
Web: www.jewishtranscript.com

Journal of Business
429 E. Third Ave.
Spokane, WA 99202
P: 509-456-5257
F: 509-4556-0624
Web: www.spokanejournal.com

Journal of the San Juans
P.O. Box 519
Friday Harbor, WA 98250
P: 360-378-4191

Lynden Tribune
P.O. Box 153
Lynden, WA 98264-9903
P: 360-354-4444
F: 360-354-4445
Web: www.lyndentrib.com

Marysville Globe
8213 State St.
Marysville, WA 98270
P: 360-659-1300

Medium
P.O. Box 22047
Seattle, WA 98122
P: 206-323-3070

Mercer Island Reporter
P.O. Box 38
Mercer Island, WA 98040
P: 206-232-1215
Web: www.mi-reporter.com

Methow Valley News
P.O. Box 97
Twisp, WA 98856
P: 509-997-7011
Web: www.methowvalley
news.com

Monroe Monitor/Valley News
P.O. Box 399
Monroe, WA 98272
P: 360-794-7116
F: 360-794-6202
Web: www.monroemonitor.com

News-Journal
600 S. Washington
Kent, WA 98031
P: 206-872-6600

News-Miner
P.O. Box 438
Republic, WA 99166
P: 509-775-3558

Nisqually Valley News
P.O. Box 597
Yelm, WA 98597
P: 360-458-2681
F: 360-458-5741
Web: www.nisquallyvalley
online.com

North Kitsap Herald
P.O. Box 278
Poulsbo, WA 98370
P: 360-779-4464
F: 360-779-8276
Web: www.northkitsap
herald.com

**Northern Kittitas
County Tribune**
221 Pennsylvania Ave.
Cle Elum, WA 98922
P: 509-674-2511
Web: www.wnpa.com

Northshore Citizen
P.O. Box 90130
Bellevue, WA 98009-9230
P: 425-486-1231
F: 425-452-3022
Web: www.northshore
citizen.com

Northwest Garden News
P.O. Box 18313
Seattle, WA 98118
P: 206-725-2394
F: 206-723-6353

Northwest Yachting
5206 Ballard N.W.
Seattle, WA 98107
P: 206-789-8116

NW Asian Weekly
P.O. Box 3468
Seattle, WA 98114
P: 206-223-0626
Web: www.nwasianweekly.com

Oceanedge
8423 S. 19th
Tacoma, WA 98466
P: 206-564-5515

Omak Chronicle
P.O. Box 553
Omak, WA 98841
P: 509-826-1110
F: 509-826-5819
Web: www.omakchronicle.com

Othello Outlook
P.O. Box O
Othello, WA 99344
P: 509-488-3342

Outlook
P.O. Box 455
Sedro Woolley, WA 98284
P: 360-855-1306

Peninsula Daily News
P.O. Box 1330
Port Angeles, WA 98362
P: 360-452-2345
P: 800-826-7714
Web: www.peninsuladaily
news.com

Peninsula Gateway
3555 Erickson St.
Gig Harbor, WA 98335
P: 253-851-9921
F: 253-851-3939
Web: www.gateline.com

**Pierce County
Business Examiner**
3123 56th St. N.W., Ste. 6
Gig Harbor, WA 98335-1311
Pike Place Market News
93 Pike St., Ste. 312
Seattle, WA 98101
P: 206-587-0351
F: 206-624-6960
Web: www.pikeplacemarket.com

**Port Townsend and
Jefferson County Leader**
P.O. Box 552
Port Townsend, WA 98368-0552
P: 360-385-2900
F: 360-385-2900
Web: www.ptleader.com

Prosser Record-Bulletin
P.O. Box 750
Prosser, WA 99350
P: 509-786-1711
Web: www.wnpa.com

Queen Anne News
225 W. Galer
Seattle, WA 98119
P: 206-461-1384
Web: www.zwire.com

Quincy Valley Post-Register
P.O. Box 217
Quincy, WA 98848
P: 509-787-4511

Reflector
P.O. Box 2020
Battle Ground, WA 98604
P: 360-687-5151
F: 360-687-5162
Web: www.thereflector.com

Seattle Post Intelligencer
101 Elliott Ave. W.
Seattle, WA 98119
P: 206-448-8000

Seattle Times
P.O. Box 70
Seattle, WA 98111
P: 206-464-2111
F: 206-464-2261
Web: www.seattletimes.nw
source.com

Seattle Weekly
1008 Western Ave.
Seattle, WA 98104
P: 206-623-0500
F: 206-467-4338
Web: www.seattleweekly.com

Shelton-Mason County Journal
P.O. Box 430
Shelton, WA 98584
P: 360-426-4412
Web: www.wnpa.com

Skagit Valley Herald
P.O. Box 578
Mount Vernon, WA 98273-5624
P: 360-336-3251
F: 360-424-5300
Web: www.news.mywebpal.com

Skamania County Pioneer
P.O. Box 250
Stevenson, WA 98648
P: 509-427-8444
Web: www.wnpa.com

Snohomish County Tribune
P.O. Box 499
Snohomish, WA 98290
P: 360-568-4121
F: 360-568-1484
Web: www.snoho.com

South County Citizen
c/o Northshore Citizen
Bothell, WA 98041
P: 206-486-1231

South County Journal
600 S. Washington
Kent, WA 98032
P: 253-872-6600
F: 253-854-1006
Web: www.southcounty
journal.com

South Whidbey Record
P.O. Box 10
Oak Harbor, WA 98277
P: 360-675-6611
Web: www.whidbeynews
times.com

Stanwood/Camano News
P.O. Box 999
Stanwood, WA 98292
P: 360-629-2155
Web: www.scnews.com

Statesman-Examiner
220 S. Main St.
Colville, WA 99114
P: 509-684-4567

Tacoma Daily Index
1019 Pacific Ave., Ste. 1216
Tacoma, WA 98402
P: 206-627-4853
Web: www.tacomadaily
index.com

Tacoma News Tribune
P.O. Box 11000
Tacoma, WA 98411-0008
P: 253-597-8742
Web: www.tribnet.com

Tenino Independent and Sun News
297 Sussex Ave. W.
Tenino, WA 98589
P: 360-264-2500

The Chewalah Independent
P.O. Box 5
Chewalah, WA 99109
P: 509-935-8422

The Chronicle
P.O. Box 88
Aberdeen, WA 98520

The Columbian
P.O. Box 180
Vancouver, WA 98666-0180
P: 360-694-3391
F: 360-699-6029
Web: www.columbian.com

The Daily Chronicle
P.O. Box 580
Centralia, WA 98531
P: 360-736-3311
P: 800-562-6084
F: 360-736-4796
Web: www.chronline.com

The Daily News
P.O. Box 189
Longview, WA 98632
P: 360-577-2571
F: 360-577-2536
F: 360-577-2536
Web: www.tdn.com

The East County Journal
P.O. Drawer M
Morton, WA 98356
P: 360-496-5993
F: 360-496-5110
Web: www.devaul
publishing.com

The Edmonds View
1827 160th Ave. N.E.
Bellevue, WA 98008-2506

**The Enumclaw
Courier-Herald**
P.O. Box 157
Enumclaw, WA 98022
P: 360-825-2555
Web: www.news.mywebpal.com

The Herald
P.O. Box 930
Everett, WA 98206
P: 425-339-3000
F: 425-339-3017
Web: www.heraldnet.com

The Issaquah Press
P.O. Box 1328
Issaquah, WA 98027
P: 425-392-6434
F: 425-391-1541
Web: www.isspress.com

The Leavenworth Echo
P.O. Box 39
Leavenworth, WA 98826
P: 509-548-4789
F: 509-782-9074
Web: www.leavenworth
echo.com

The New Times
P.O. Box 51186
Seattle, WA 98115-1186
P: 206-320-7788
F: 206-320-7717
Web: www.newtimes.org

The Odessa Record
1 W. First Ave.
Odessa, WA 99159
P: 509-982-2632
Web: www.wnpa.com

The Olympian
P.O. Box 407
Olympia, WA 98507
P: 360-754-5400
Web: www.theolympian.com

The Ritzville Adams County Journal
P.O. Box 288
Ritzville, WA 99169
P: 509-659-1020
Web: www.wnpa.com

The Seattle Medium
2600 S. Jackson
Seattle, WA 98144
P: 206-632-3307
Web: www.seattlemedium.
blackpressusa.com

The Spokesman-Review
P.O. Box 2160
Spokane, WA 99210
P: 509-459-5000
Web: www.spokesman
review.com

The Sprague Advocate
P.O. Box 327
Sprague, WA 99032
P: 509-257-2311

The Standard-Register
P.O. Box 988
Tekoa, WA 99033
P: 509-284-5782

The Star
P.O. Box 150
Grand Coulee, WA 99133

P: 509-633-1350
Web: www.zwire.com

The Sun
P.O. Box 259
Bremerton, WA 98337
P: 360-377-3711
Web: www.thesunlink.com

The Tribune
P.O. Box 400
Deer Park, WA 99006
P: 509-276-5043
F: 509-276-2041
Web: www.wnpa.com

The Waitsburg Times
P.O. Box 97
Waitsburg, WA 99361-0097
P: 509-337-6631
Web: www.wnpa.com

The Wapato Independent
P.O. Box 67
Wapato, WA 98951
P: 509-877-3322

The Wenatchee World
P.O. Box 1511
Wenatchee, WA 98807-1511
P: 509-663-5161
F: 509-662-5413
Web: www.wenworld.com

Toppenish Review
P.O. Box 511
Toppenish, WA 98948
P: 509-865-4055
Web: www.wnpa.com

Tri-City Herald
107 N. Cascade St.
Kennewick, WA 99336
P: 509-582-1500
P: 800-874-0445
Web: www.tri-cityherald.com

Union-Bulletin
P.O. Box 1358
Walla Walla, WA 99362
P: 509-525-3300
P: 800-423-5617
Web: www.zwire.com

Valley News Herald
P.O. Box 142020
Spokane, WA 99214
P: 509-924-2440
Web: www.spokanevalley
online.com

Vashon Beachcomber
P.O. Box 447
Vashon, WA 98070
P: 206-463-9195
Web: www.vashonbeach
comber.com

**Wahkiakum County
Eagle/Washington
Newspaper Pub. Assoc.**
3838 Stone Way North
Seattle, WA 98103
P: 206-634-3838
F: 206-634-3842
Web: www.wnpa.com

**Washington Teamster
Newspaper**
552 Denny Way
Seattle, WA 98109
P: 206-622-0483

Whidbey News Times
P.O. Box 10
Oak Harbor, WA 98277
P: 360-675-6611
Web: www.whidbeynews
times.com

White Salmon Enterprise
P.O. Box 218
White Salmon, WA 98672
P: 509-493-2112
Web: www.whitesalmon
enterprise.com

Wilbur Register
P.O. Box 186
Wilbur, WA 99185
P: 509-647-5551
Web: www.wnpa.com

**Woodinville Weekly
Northlake**
P.O. Box 587
Woodinville, WA 98072
P: 206-483-0606

Yakima Herald-Republic
P.O. Box 9668
Yakima, WA 98901
P: 509-452-7533
Web: www.yakima-herald.com

University Presses

Any directory of Northwest publishers would not be complete without including the university presses of the Northwest.

Since Cornell University president, Andrew D. White opened their press in 1869 American universities have recognized the opportunities and advantages of university "publishing."

University presses often help keep prominent local authors in print and encourage new writers.

They publish poetry and creative non-fiction and build a sense of local community and pride in regional achievement.

In 2000 there were ninety-two university presses in the United States and Canada publishing approximately 11,000 books.

The following Northwest university presses currently produce quality books.

Eastern Washington University Press
705 West First Avenue
Spokane, WA 99201

Oregon State Press
101 Waldo Hall
Corvallis, Or 97331-6407
P: (541) 737-3166
E: osu.press@oregonstate.edu
Founded in 1961— Publishes 15 books a year.

University of Alaska Press
P.O. Box 756240
Fairbanks, AK 99775
The University of Alaska Press traces its origins to a biography published in 1927 Mines. From the 1920s to the early 1980s, the press was relatively dormant but still published thirteen titles. The University of Alaska's Board of Regents formally recognized the press' existence in 1979.

University of Idaho Press
P.O. Box 444416
Moscow, ID 83844-4416
P: (208) 885-3300
Founded in 1972.

University of Oregon Press
5283 University of Oregon
Eugene, OR 97403-5283
P: 541-683-3216
Founded in 1920s. Imprint curtailed in 1970s. Press reinvigorated recently for the 125th anniversary of University of Oregon founding.

University of Nevada Press
Mail Stop 166
Reno, NV 89557-0076
P: 877-682-6657

**University of
Washington Press**
1326 Fifth Avenue, Suite 555
Seattle, WA 98101-2604
P: 206- 543-4050

The first book to bear the
U of W Press appeared in 1920.
They publish about 60 new
titles a year.

Washington State Press
P.O. Box 645910
Pullman, WA 99164-5910
P: 509-335-3518
Web: www.wsu.edu/wsupress

Advertisers

Oregon Writers Colony

A nonprofit organization representing and nurturing professional and novice writers. Founded in 1983 in Portland, Oregon.

In 1989, OWC purchased a large log home perched on a ridge in Rockaway Beach, Ore., overlooking the Pacific Ocean to the West and Lake Lytle to the East, and named it Colonyhouse. It is a writer's haven, for members only.

OWC activities and member benefits:

• Conferences and workshops to further professional growth. Open to all; reduced fees for members. Many workshops and seminars take place at Colonyhouse year-round.

• OWC Presents! A series of workshops for writers, held at Powell's Books, Cascade Plaza, Beaverton (across Hwy. 217 from Washington Square). Open to all.
7 p.m. on 4th Monday of the month.

• Spring Conference, held at the unique writers' retreat—Sylvia Beach Hotel—in Newport, Ore. The entire hotel is reserved for participants, with meals and rooms included in conference fee.

• Annual Fiction and Nonfiction Short Story Contest with monetary prizes awarded.

• The Colonygram: a bimonthly newsletter for writers

• Website: www.oregonwriterscolony.org

• Membership fees: Annual–$35; Patron–$100 year; Life Membership–$500.

> **For information:**
> **Phone:** 503-827-8072
> **Email**: www.oregonwriterscolony.org
> **Write to:** P.O. Box 15200, Portland OR 97293-5200

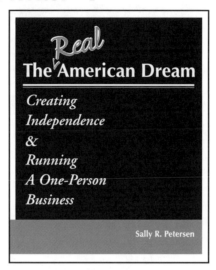

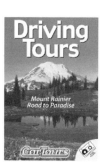

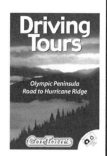

Don't judge a book by its cover.

As a writer, you know how clichés can be so, well… trite.

They're also frequently **not true.**

Make sure your next book is properly judged.

Media Weavers, *L.L.C.*

7th Edition Writers Northwest Handbook
and
Writers Northwest Quarterly
Order Information

Name _____

Title/Org _____

Address _____

_____
City   State   Zip

Telephone _____

Email _____

1 year subscription (4 issues), $10.00 $_____
Writers Northwest Quarterly

Number of copies _____ Hardcover, $22.95 $_____
7th Edition Writers Northwest Handbook

            Shipping and handling $3.00 per book $_____

               TOTAL AMOUNT ENCLOSED $_____

Please mail check or money order with this form to:

    Media Weavers L.L.C.
    P.O. Box 86190
    Portland, OR 97286

Please allow 3-4 weeks for delivery.

mediaweavers@attbi.com

"Success comes to a writer, as a rule,

so gradually that it is always

something of a shock to him

to look back and realize

the heights to which he has climbed."

P.G. Wodehouse